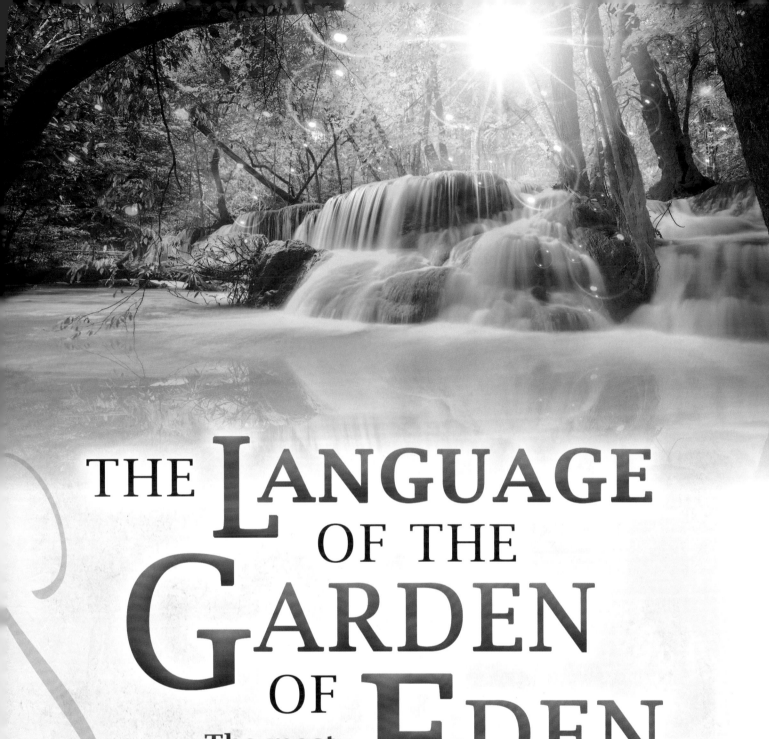

The Language OF THE Garden OF Eden

The most important message ever communicated to humanity

C.J. LOVIK

www.rockislandbooks.com

Visit our website
to purchase books and preview
upcoming titles.

Contact us at:
feedback@rockislandbooks.com

Cover Design and Interior Layout by Sergio E. León

Sergio was born and raised in Mexico City, where he studied Design and Arts in the National Autonomous University of Mexico (UNAM). For more than 23 years, Sergio has worked in a variety of positions, primarily acting as Art and Design Director for major brands and publications. Today, Sergio is the Art and Design Director for Lighthouse Gospel Beacon, where he is responsible for all digital and print media. Every day, Sergio is growing in Christ while continuing to produce art and media to help illustrate the love of the Savior. Sergio is married to his wonderful wife, Monica, and they have two amazing children.

Table of Contents

CHAPTER 1

The Language of Eden

This book is about the most important message ever communicated to man.

Happily, we have a trustworthy English translation of the revelation preserved in the Hebrew Scriptures.

We all know that this revelation was originally written in an ancient language.

Few have considered that this ancient language pre-dates all other languages on the earth. Even fewer have deeply considered the history of this language from a biblical perspective.

If you take the time to learn the twenty-two "letters" in the modern Hebrew Aleph-Beyt, you would find it difficult to perceive the majority of ancient pictographs that originally were the foundations for each of the current modern Hebrew symbols.

Take a look at the modern Hebrew script that composes the 22 letter Aleph-Beyt, and see if you can discern the original ancient pictographs that these modern symbols replaced.

ח	ז	ו	ה	ד	ג	ב	א
CHET 8	ZAYIN 7	VAV 6	HEY 5	DALET 4	GIMEL 3	BEYT 2	ALEPH 1
ע	ס	נ	מ	ל	כ	י	ט
AYIN 16	SAMECH 15	NOON 14	MEM 13	LAMED 12	KAF 11	YOOD 10	TET 9
ת	ש	ר	ק	צ	פ		
TAV 22	SHEEN 21	REYSH 20	QOOF 19	TSADE 18	PEY 17		

Most western readers, at this point, are probably tempted to close the book and move on to something they can more readily get their heads around.

The Hebrew language does look a little daunting.

I do understand that you might be wondering if you're in over your head. I certainly thought so when I began to investigate this over a decade ago.

If you're having doubts about going forward with this investigation, I would like to encourage you with this simple promise: *Before you finish this chapter, you will be able to identify the meaning of each and every one of the letters in the Hebrew Aleph-Beyt.*

I make this promise because I know it is true.

As a matter of fact, a child eight or more years of age without any prior knowledge or familiarity with Hebrew language will be able to identify at first glance the majority of these symbols. And, after a brief explanation they will be able to identify them effortlessly.

It is at this point that we begin our investigation of the most amazing "hidden in plain sight" revelatory miracles to be re-discovered in the 21st century.

I now invite you to take a look at what is commonly known as the Proto-Canaanite language. This is the language that we know as *Hebrew.*

While the term Proto-Canaanite is helpful, it does not convey the full history of the language we know today as Hebrew — a language that predates King David, Joshua, Moses, Abraham, Noah, Enoch, and finally Seth, the son of Adam.

What you're about to view is the picture-by-picture script that was revealed by God to Moses.

This original Divine revelation was first carved into stone by Moses, copied on papyrus by the scribes, and even etched into clay tablets and pottery producing what we know as the *Torah.*

You are now looking at the original pictographs that accurately display what Moses chiseled into stone to produce what we now know as the first five books of the Bible starting with Genesis and ending with Deuteronomy.

Now, you're probably wondering how we can know this with 100% certainty.

That is a very important question and one that will be thoroughly answered in this book. I cannot take credit for discovering the answer to this question because it was only my curiosity and a bit of sleuthing that easily uncovered the one thing that holds all of this together.

What is that one thing?

Why it is God, the revelator, of course.

He in His wisdom has solved this issue so there can be no dispute about it.

It is almost as if He knew ahead of time that there would be several ways you could hide this revelation, and He made sure that could not happen. I am speaking tongue-in-cheek as obviously God did preserve the foundational under-pinings of His first revelation to mankind.

You will laugh when you learn how He did it. It is **PURE GENIUS!**

You can look forward to reading all about it as you study this book. This is just one more gem to be put in your pocket as a reward for persevering into what only looks like a daunting investigation.

In the end, you will discover that this revelation was not designed to intrigue the scholars or great minds of the east and west. There is no hidden code to be unlocked by some incantation of the Hebrew letters as is falsely imagined by the would-be magicians that call themselves *Kabbalists*.

This is so simple a child can understand it and perhaps that is exactly the audience God had in view.

So, please continue this quest with the promise that you will be rewarded with the keys that will allow you to unlock the heart and mind of God in ways you never thought possible. This is no intrusion into the mystery of

God. It has been revealed as an invitation so that you might know Him, and to know Him is to love Him, as He intended you to do.

You will discover nothing unorthodox in this book. Everything you will learn simply amplifies and magnifies the over-arching theme of God's revelation.

And, what is that majestic theme?

It is His Son the Messiah, Jesus the Christ, who is the only begotten Son of God — God Incarnate!

Now, take a few minutes to look at the original pictures or pictographs that were revealed to Moses symbol-by-symbol. This is God's language revealed to mankind. You will notice one addition. A good teacher always looks for ways to layer in new information that is foundational to the teaching. I will try my best to be a good teacher.

In the original picture, God assigned a number to each of the Hebrew pictographs. He did this in order to magnify the revelation. So, what you're looking at is not a modern addition as it was present from the beginning and included in the revelation we call the Old Testament.

The numbers go from 1 to 10 then 20 to 100 then finally 100 to 400.

The very first decimal system was not invented by the Persians but by God Himself.

What do these numbers mean?

The answer will be explored more fully as you go forward, but the easiest way to understand it is that the numbers were a progressive revelation based on how those numbers were used in the holy Scriptures, from Genesis through Revelation.

Some of those numbers are easy to understand and their meaning is known by most Christians. The number **3** has the meaning of **DIVINE**

PERFECTION, number **7 DIVINE COMPLETION, 10 ORDINAL PERFECTION**, and **12 GOVERNMENTAL PERFECTION.** These four numbers are well known and have been called "Sacred Numbers" as they have special significance that is well understood.

In addition, the number **5** is commonly known as the number of **GRACE.** The number **40** is known as the number of **TESTING & PROBATION.** The number **50** is known as the number of **JUBILEE.**

The number **100** is well known as the number of **PROMISE** to the Children of Israel. (Remember that Abraham was 100 years old when the Child of Promise, ISAAC, was born.)

There are many well-trusted and popular study books on the topic of the spiritual significance of numbers. Most prominently, I would invite you to investigate the published works of the following men who have done a great job of faithfully uncovering the spiritual significance of numbers, as they are used in the Holy Bible and in the Bible alone. (E.W. Bullinger) No outside sources are used.

Now, let's take a look at the language of the Garden of Eden, the language we know today as Hebrew. The only pure language in the world. That is not my opinion, it is God's. Read what God told Zephaniah, the prophet. This would be the language spoken by the children of Israel when God returned them to Israel after they had been scattered.

ZEPHANIAH 3:9
For then will I turn to the people a pure language, that they may all call upon the name of the Lord, to serve him with one consent.

How many of the following symbols can you easily identify?

Most people without any aid can figure out at least 10 of the 22.

See how many you can identify before reading the list at the bottom of the chart.

CHET 8	ZAYIN 7	VAV 6	HEY 5	DALET 4	GIMEL 3	BEYT 2	ALEPH 1
AYIN 16/70	SAMECH 15/60	NOON 14/50	MEM 13/40	LAMED 12/30	KAF 11/20	YOOD 10	TET 9
TAV 22/400	SHEEN 21/300	REYSH 20/200	QOOF 19/100	TSADE 18/90	PEY 17/80		

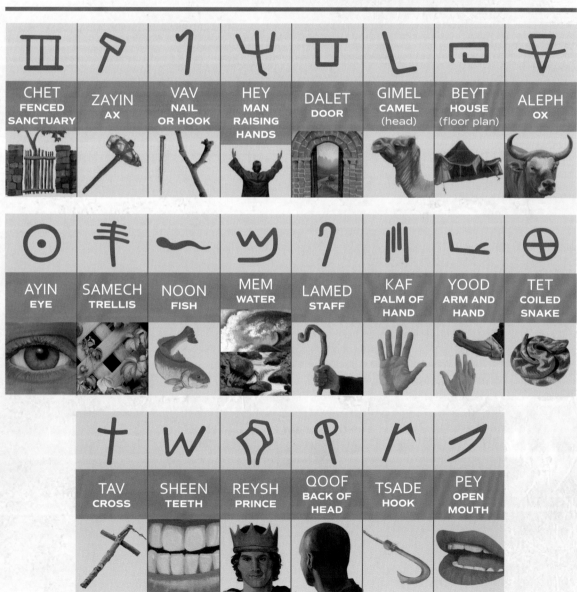

CHET FENCED SANCTUARY	ZAYIN AX	VAV NAIL OR HOOK	HEY MAN RAISING HANDS	DALET DOOR	GIMEL CAMEL (head)	BEYT HOUSE (floor plan)	ALEPH OX

AYIN EYE	SAMECH TRELLIS	NOON FISH	MEM WATER	LAMED STAFF	KAF PALM OF HAND	YOOD ARM AND HAND	TET COILED SNAKE

TAV CROSS	SHEEN TEETH	REYSH PRINCE	QOOF BACK OF HEAD	TSADE HOOK	PEY OPEN MOUTH

So, now that you have completed this exercise, I think you will agree that the symbols and their pictographic meaning are present in the ancient language of the Garden of Eden.

However, you're probably wondering who decided what some of the less obvious pictures meant?

It is pretty clear that Tav † is a picture of Crossed Wooden Sticks.

It is not as obvious that Gimel ∟ is a Camel. Who decided that the symbol of Gimel was a symbol of a Camel and not a leaning tree or a giraffe?

The answer, as disclosed earlier, is that **GOD** decided!

How exactly did God work that out?

How can we be sure that the pictures have remained the same after over 6000 years from the time God gifted Adam with the phonetic, picture and number language we know today as Hebrew?

The answer is eloquently simple.

God named each symbol. The name each symbol bears is either the name or the ancient root of the Hebrew name of the picture. This is not speculation. It is a linguistic and historical matter of fact.

CHAPTER 2

Hebrew Letters are Also Words

No other language in the world has survived for 6000, or even 3000 years. Only God's pure language has been *miraculously* preserved. This proves at least a dozen things that are important. I would like you to consider just one of these things.

God preserved the language of the Garden of Eden in order that you might explore its majesty, power, and message. He did it for you and me, Adam's children 6000 years removed. He did it for us.

Is there a revelation contained in each word that amplifies the meaning of each of the 22 symbols in the Hebrew Aleph-Beyt? **ABSOLUTELY.**

That will be the subject of another book.

For now, simply marvel at the fact that God preserved the very foundational pictures that make up each Hebrew word picture. Marvel that these are pictures everybody can identify, even 6000 years later.

Can you even imagine the planning and wisdom that went into what you are about to examine?

Just thinking about it sends chills up and down my spine. I hope it has the same awesome effect on you.

Original Ancient Hebrew Word or Root Word that illustrates each of the 22 Symbols (Script) that compose the Hebrew Aleph-Beyt

(Remember that Hebrew is written from RIGHT to LEFT)

The Three Symbol Word **ALEPH** *means* **OX**
(Read Right to Left)

Pey	Lamed	ALEPH

The Three Symbol Word **BEYT** *means* **HOUSE or TENT**

Tav	Yood	BEYT

The Four Symbol Word **GIMEL** *means* **CAMEL**

Lamed	Mem	Yood	GIMEL

The Three Symbol Word **DALET** *means* **DOOR**

Tav	Lamed	**DALET**

The Two Symbol Word **HEY** *means* **TO BEHOLD**

Aleph	**HEY**

The Two Symbol Word **VAV** *means* **HOOK & NAIL**

Vav	**VAV**

The Three Symbol Word **ZAYIN** *means* **AX**

Noon	Yood	ZAYIN

The Three Symbol Word **CHET** *means* **SANCTUARY**

Tav	Yood	CHET

The Three Symbol Word **TET** *means* **SNAKE**

Tav	Yood	TET

*The Three Symbol Word **YOOD** means **ARM & HAND***

Dalet	Vav	YOOD
⊓	۲	ﬥ

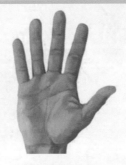

*The Two Symbol Word **KAF** means **PALM of HAND***

Pey	KAF
↗	ⱴ

*The Three Symbol Word **LAMED** means **STAFF***

Dalet	Mem	LAMED
⊓	ⱳ	۲

The Two Symbol Word **MEM** *means* **LIQUID or WATER**

Mem	MEM

The Three Symbol Word **NOON** *means* **SPROUT or FISH**

Noon	Vav	NOON

The Three Symbol Word **SAMECH** *means* **TRELLIS or PROP**

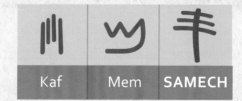

Kaf	Mem	SAMECH

The Three Symbol Word **AYIN** *means* **EYE**

| Noon | Yood | AYIN |

The Two Symbol Word **PEY** *means* **MOUTH**

| Aleph | PEY |

The Three Symbol Word **TSADE** *means* **HOOK**

| Yood | Dalet | TSADE |

The Three Symbol Word **QOOF** *means* **BACK of HEAD**

Pey	Vav	QOOF

The Three Symbol Word **REYSH** *means* **HEAD PERSON**

Sheen	Yood	REYSH

The Three Symbol Word **SHEEN** *means* **TEETH**

Noon	Yood	SHEEN

*The Two Symbol Word **TAV** means **CROSS***

God Himself preserved the meaning of the symbols so that even if they were modified, as He knew they would be, the picture would remain for those who took the time and effort to figure it out. This is not difficult to do.

There are three facts that are indisputable and the foundational bedrock of this book.

1. The first language gifted to Adam is actually three languages in one. It was **FIRST** a **PHONETIC LANGUAGE** to be used in the same conventional way that any language, including English, is used. Concepts are imbedded in words that are then used as the foundational basis of communication. The language of the Garden of Eden was a **PHONETIC LANGUAGE.**

2. The language gifted to Adam was **SECONDLY** a picture language. It was first translated into script for the purpose of communicating by way of writing as a **PICTOGRAPHIC LANGUAGE.** The difference between the Aleph-Beyt of the Language of the Garden and English is simple. In English you learn phonetic words made up of letters that have an agreed upon meaning. The word *apple* in English is a combination of five

letters that we learn mean an apple. The Language of the Garden is made up of individual pictures that are displayed as pictographs or symbols that are learned in order to compose a concept based on each picture. God has preserved this picture in order that we might investigate them with humility and reverence.

③ The language gifted to Adam was **THIRDLY** a **NUMERIC LANGUAGE**. A language that was meant to be investigated numerically as it yielded up its meaning as the revelation of the Scriptures progressed. We now have the complete revelation and the complete record of how God used numbers for His prophetic purposes.

These are the three principle facts that give us courage to carefully and humbly explore the meaning of not only the phonetic revelation but also the pictorial and the numeric revelations. Together they are self-authenticating, magnifying, and amplifying levels of Divine revelation. They are all in harmony with one another in order to declare God's Divine supernatural purposes for his entire creation. A creation that is even now groaning for the manifestation of the sons of God.

Let's add one more element to the 22 pictographs we call the Hebrew Aleph-Beyt.

This is done for the purpose of locking into your mind the pictures that God placed in front of the first man to see them, Moses, and all who followed up to the time of Daniel the prophet. While Daniel was a captive in Babylon, the Hebrew pictograms you see in the next chapter were *modified* or *updated* by the Hebrew Scribes who were banished to Babylon for their idolatry and unbelief.

CHAPTER 3

The Timeless Pure Language of the Garden *updated* in Babylon

(Illustrations added)

Early Hebrew Pictograms (Script)
Pre-Babylonian Captivity

(Hebrew that Abraham, Moses, David, and the Prophets could read.)

CHET 8	ZAYIN 7	VAV 6	HEY 5	DALET 4	GIMEL 3	BEYT 2	ALEPH 1

AYIN 16/70	SAMECH 15/60	NOON 14/50	MEM 13/40	LAMED 12/30	KAF 11/20	YOOD 10	TET 9

TAV 22/400	SHEEN 21/300	REYSH 20/200	QOOF 19/100	TSADE 18/90	PEY 17/80

OX, HOUSE (floor plan), CAMEL (head), DOOR, MAN RAISING HANDS, NAIL or HOOK, AX, FENCED SANCTUARY

COILED SNAKE, ARM and HAND, PALM of HAND, STAFF, WATER, FISH, TRELLIS

EYE, OPEN MOUTH, HOOK, BACK OF HEAD, PRINCE, TEETH, CROSS

Look Again with Fresh Eyes

Let's take another look at the pictures embedded in each Hebrew letter as we consider the genius of God's chosen method of communication with sinful and fallen mankind.

An Ox is always an Ox

The symbol or picture of the Ox might change from 𐤀 (proto-Canaanite) to 𐤀 (Moses) based on the medium used to scribe the pictogram, but the concept is retained in both symbols.

It became a matter of settling on which symbol to use in order to promote unity without deviation. Once used, it would become a well understood and accepted tradition.

Everyone knew what the symbol meant; Aleph was always an Ox and there was not one other of the 22 letters that could be confused with it.

Newer is not always better!

I do not know what or who "inspired" the Scribes, who were taken into captivity in Babylon, to alter the Hebrew Aleph-Beyt in order to conform it to the Aramaic Block Script. Perhaps, they thought it would be a good idea to *modernize* the ancient Aleph-Beyt to be in line with the script used by the rest of the nations.

Hasn't this always been one of Israel's problems?

Perhaps, it was an attempt by Satan to sabotage the revelation of Scripture or at least make it more difficult to trace its origins back to its ancient and original roots. This was malevolently motivated by the fact that these original roots were bathing in the pure water of God's revelation.

Or, perhaps there is a more innocent explanation.

Whatever the reason, the results are obvious.

A barrier has been erected that makes it more difficult to apprehend the pictures that were embedded in the Hebrew letters.

Obviously, the changes did not completely obscure the original pictures, but they did alter the original pictures in a way that now requires an extra layer of information in order to discover the root picture meaning of Hebrew words.

Can you identify the Picture that is "Hidden" in the Modern Hebrew Script?

We invite you to take the challenge.

Can you find the Crossed Wooden Sticks, the Gated Sanctuary, and the Man Looking Up pictured in the Modern Hebrew Script?

CROSS
Garden Gated Sanctuary
Looking Up

How many did you get right?

Now, do the same test as you observe the early Hebrew pictograms.

CROSS

Garden Gated Sanctuary

Looking Up

| Chet | Hey | Tav |

As you can see, the early Hebrew pictograms, which were in use up until the Babylonian captivity, were pretty simple to figure out. And, once learned, a child could write and remember them with ease.

Remembering details is high on God's list of things He wanted man to master.

The pictographic Hebrew retained an obvious connection between the symbol and what it was symbolizing up until the Babylonian captivity.

Torah Scroll
Unrolled to Exodus 3b, referencing
the building of the tabernacle.
In Hebrew
Gevil
Persia
1800s
MOTB.SCR.003630

Reading Table
Podiums used for Torah reading have
taken many shapes and forms.
Wood
Poland
1907
GC FUR 000122

From that point in time, we are told to forget the old as it no longer has meaning.

Who decided that?

You be the Judge!

I would like you to consider 11 of the 22 early pictograms.

How long do you think it would take to learn them?

Here is a sampling of the early symbols. How long would it take you to make the connection between the pictogram and the object it represents?

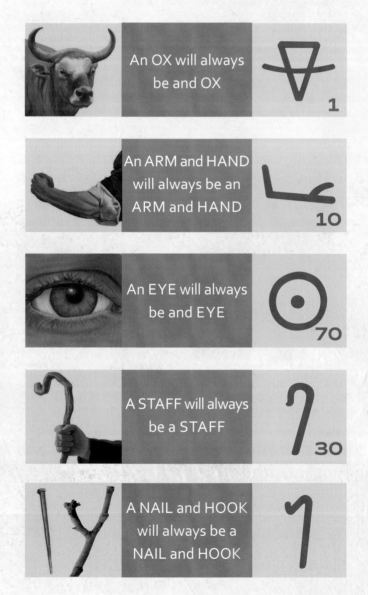

	An OX will always be and OX	1
An ARM and HAND will always be an ARM and HAND	10
An EYE will always be and EYE	70
A STAFF will always be a STAFF	30
A NAIL and HOOK will always be a NAIL and HOOK	

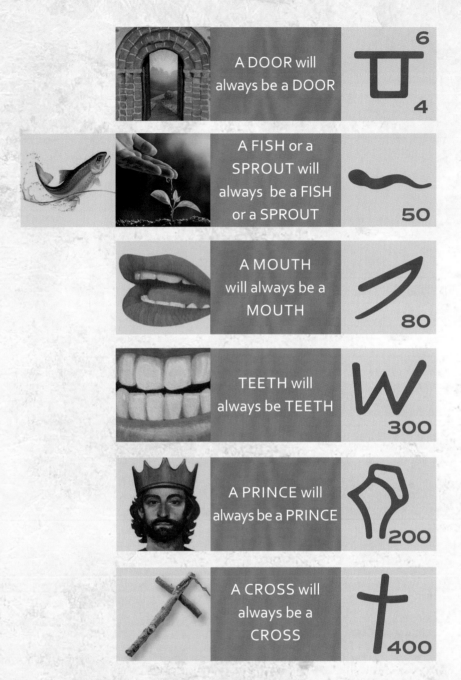

A DOOR will always be a DOOR		6 / 4
A FISH or a SPROUT will always be a FISH or a SPROUT		50
A MOUTH will always be a MOUTH		80
TEETH will always be TEETH		300
A PRINCE will always be a PRINCE		200
A CROSS will always be a CROSS		400

And now you know why we us the ancient Hebrew symbols!

The supernatural perspective, that is the bedrock foundation of this book, is informed by the ancient prophetic Scriptures that we call the Old and New Testament.

We believe that the living Word of God was the only thing that left the Garden of Eden unmolested after the treachery of sin and rebellion entered into the heart of Adam.

The language of the Garden of Eden is a miraculous language that contains the seed plot for all human existence and cradles the one hope, the only hope, that mankind can reliably depend upon.

I do not believe, and could never be persuaded to believe, that **THE WORD OF GOD** was birthed in the belly of the "Beast of Babylon" in the Valley of Shinar, during the Satanic reign of Nimrod.

I do not believe the Hebrew language is the step-child of the corrupted post-Babel languages of the Phoenicians, Akkadians, and Egyptians.

CHAPTER 4

Seeing is Believing

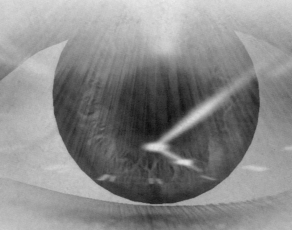

Even when modified to conform to the modern block Aramaic language, the language of the Babylonian captivity, the core integrity of the letters is preserved.

The final proof is in the ancient Hebrew text, in the symbols and in the numbers.

Do they yield nonsense and confusion when they are examined by God's children?

Or, are they a source of comfort and encouragement consistent with the biblical revelation?

Does the simple picture language magnify God and His only begotten Son?

Do you hear the Master's voice amplified in the simple pictures and numbers that foundationally compose the Hebrew words?

Is there anything in the pictures or numbers that is in conflict with the phonetic revelation we know as conventional Hebrew? A language that God has graciously given us so that we might discover His Son, in order that we might be delivered from the wrath of God.

There has always been a remnant that believed, cherished, and published the message. But, sadly, the very people who were separated out of all the nations and commissioned to make the message known to the entire world have themselves been blinded in part to the purpose and power of the revelation.

This book is a call to men of faith to rediscover the majesty and power of the first revelation God gifted man. The revelation was miraculously gifted to the first man, Adam, in order that he might have fellowship and communion with his Creator. This language was not learned but bestowed on the mind of Adam in order that Adam might know and understand the mind and heart of God.

The Language of the Garden of Eden is a language like no other.

It is a language with three-parts, each magnifying and amplifying the other.

Three languages woven into one and originally communicated in somewhat the same way you might watch a silent movie with a written storyline underneath the moving picture.

This is a poor example as it does not capture the full experience that Adam must have had communicating with his Creator. But, it does get us on the path to understanding the indisputable fact that the language of the Garden of Eden was audible and phonetic, pictographic and numeric — all at the same time!

A pure language was integrated seamlessly into the uncorrupted mind of Adam. Adam was not confused by the conversations he had with God. Adam enjoyed sweet fellowship with his Creator in the cool of the evening, while residing without sin in the wonderous Garden of Eden.

And, the first task God set Adam's mind to was based on this new gift of language. Adam named **ALL** the animals.

The Garden is gone. But, one thing remains — the majestic and glorious subject of this book.

Will you be as able and capable as Adam in your understanding of the first written revelation given to mankind? A revelation revealed pictogram-by-pictogram, as we would say, letter-by-letter to Moses who scribed it just exactly as God revealed it.

The answer is "of course not". We do not have Adam's intelligence or the purity of thought given to Adam before he sinned. And, yet, the revelation remains for our investigation.

Even through our mesh of sin filters that corrupt good communication, even with our diminished intelligence, and even with our sinful nature, we can still glean the field of revelation found in the Old Testament originally written down in the language of the Garden. A language that has retained 6000 years later the very symbols and pictures that God downloaded into the mind of Adam. Pictures that remained as the pictographic text of the Holy Scriptures up until the time of the Babylonian captivity. Even with the alteration of the symbols while in Babylon, the picture God created for each letter miraculously remains by God's sovereign will to this very day.

It is my belief that we are living in the days prophesied by Daniel. This is the time of *the end* when things hidden may be finally revealed.

God's revelation has not and never will change.

What does change is man's ability to comprehend the revelation with an understanding that is supernatural in origin. If you do not believe that then please read what Jesus said as reported in the Gospel of Matthew.

The Hebrew language with its pictures all strung together with **NO** capital letters, **NO** periods, **NO** commas, or any other punctuation or separation has been translated into English based on the phonetic understanding of the text. This is, of course, part of God's gracious plan to keep His revelation in front of mankind.

If you consult a Hebrew Interlinear you can see the modern Hebrew text with spaces added to accommodate the definition of the original pictographs that have been consolidated into thoughts and expressed as words.

What if you took the time to look at the pictures that make up the individual Hebrew words? What if you re-translated those modern symbols to their original pictograms?

You would discover a picture language that even a child, a babe, could understand.

The purpose of this book is not to impress anyone with a complicated coded messaging system that can only be understood by a few.

The purpose of this book is to introduce you to a revelation that was given to man so that he might be redeemed in order to renew his fellowship and friendship with his Creator.

The message of redemption was "baked into the cake," as it were.

What will you discover when you begin examining the pictures God revealed as one of three foundations in His written revelation to man?

You will discover a revelation that has been amazingly designed to have one grand theme and one theme only.

That theme is expressed in thousands of ways, much the way a diamond reflects a thousand facets when held up to light.

What is that grand theme?

It is the magnification and amplification of the Son of God, Jesus the Christ, who became Immanuel (the God-man) in order to offer the pure blood sacrifice required to quench the wrath of God.

The theme of the entire Old Testament is Christ — the appointed one who came to save us from the wrath that will come on all those who refuse God's gracious plan of salvation, which is based on the blood sacrifice of His only begotten Son, Jesus the Christ.

This is not over-blown hyperbole. This is a fact that you will soon come in contact with if you continue to read this book. I know you have lots of questions. Since I began this journey, almost a decade ago, I have asked many of the questions on your mind. By the time you finish reading this book, I believe those questions will be addressed and answered.

At that time Jesus answered and said, I thank thee, O Father Lord (YHVH) of heaven and earth, because thou hast hid these things from the wise and prudent, and hast revealed them unto babes. Even so, Father: for so it seemed good in thy sight.

MATTHEW 11:25-26

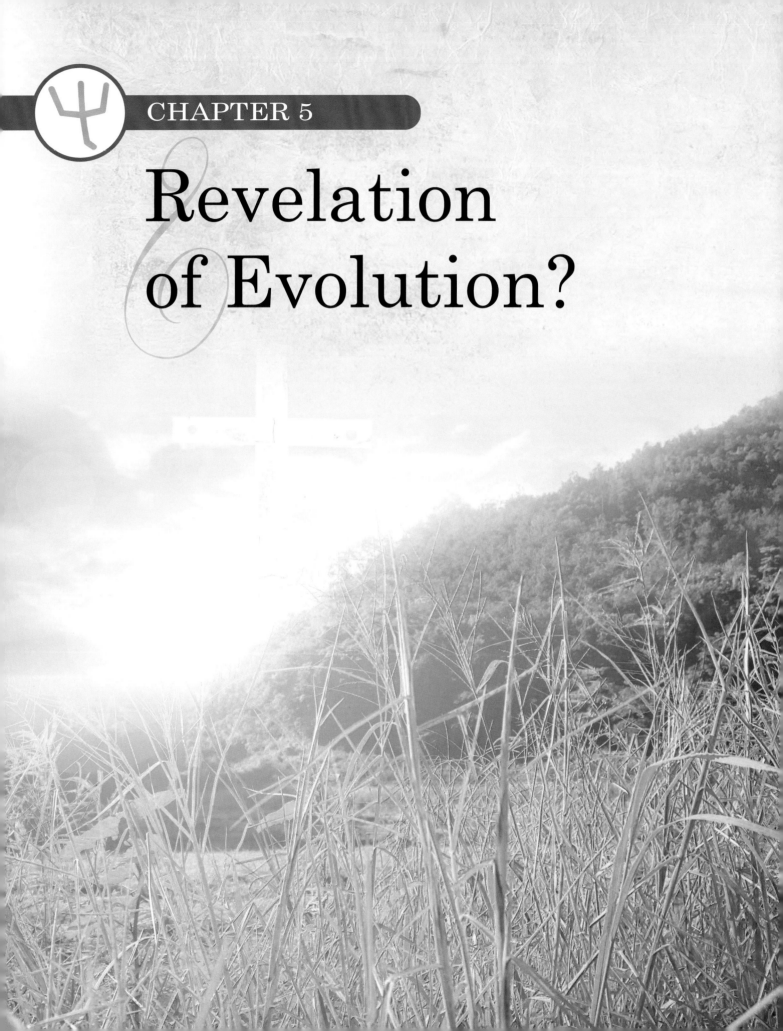

CHAPTER 5

Revelation of Evolution?

The commonly held belief, among those who deny the veracity and literal interpretation of biblical history, is that Hebrew is a simple, unsophisticated, subordinate language that evolved from the more advanced blending of the Sumerian and the Akkadian Semitic languages.

From the fusion of these two languages, we are supposed to believe the Hebrew language had its beginning.

Many, who promote this historical linguistic theory, teach that all the stories found in the first five books of the Bible were simply "borrowed" and "re-fashioned" from the myths that were prevalent in the region of Mesopotamia.

Some, who are sympathetic to the biblical account, teach that, while the events recorded in Genesis may be generally relied upon, the actual original words used to record the events wriggled out of the pagan languages that "progressively developed" in the region of Sumer, also refered to as the Plains of Shinar.

These theories deny the unique creation account found in Genesis.

Not surprisingly, most deny that there was a literal Adam and Eve.

As can be expected, those that hold the "borrowed language" theory mock the notion that Hebrew is the first language spoken on the earth.

According to this corrupted history of the earth, all things, including the Hebrew language, sprang from Sumer in Mesopotamia and are subordinate to its pagan history and mythos.

This is the anti-supernatural position taken by almost all of those who do not believe that the Scriptures are a unique divine revelation from the LORD God who made the heavens and the earth, created Adam in His own image, and gifted him with the pure uncorrupted language we know today as Hebrew.

When is the last time you met an Acadian, had lunch with an Ammonite, or celebrated Moabite Monday?

Of all the languages that fall into the category of Canaanite languages, including Phoenician, Acadian, Punic, Babylonian, Amorite, Ammonite, Moabite, Edomite, and many more, only one ancient language miraculously exists to this day.

If you believe that the ancient prophetic Scriptures are a revelation from Almighty God then you already know, based on the prophetic word, what language miraculously exists while all the other Canaanite languages are extinct.

Is Hebrew a crude unpolished language that owes its origins to the Sumerian, Egyptians, Chinese, or Phoenician pictographic languages?

As evidence that the answer is *yes*, language scholars point out the complexity of those pictographic languages and assume that Hebrew, with its simple childlike pictures, must have been an inferior "spin off" of the more sophisticated and complex pictographic languages that sprang forth as man progressed into more intelligent and technologically advanced people groups.

Only orthodox Jews and a small remnant of Christians rely on a literal interpretation of the Scriptures for their worldview. Most of those in this small subset of "biblical literalist" are convinced that all languages, including the Egyptian, Sumerian, and Chinese, while obviously similar in some ways, owe their beginning to the original language of the Garden of Eden, not the other way around.

The Miracle of Chaos and Confusion

If we take a look at this question from a biblical perspective, the history of language is clearly outlined, logical, and simple to understand.

GENESIS 11:1, 7

1 And the whole earth was of one language, and of one speech.
7 Go to, let us go down, and there confound their language, that they may not understand one another's speech.

GENESIS 11:9

Therefore is the name of it called Babel; because the Lord did there confound the language of all the earth: and from thence did the Lord scatter them abroad upon the face of all the earth.

According to the Bible, all the languages on the earth, except the language of the Garden of Eden, were confused and corrupted languages that all had miraculous beginnings at the Tower of Babel.

If you find it hard to believe that the first man, Adam, was graciously gifted with the language of the Garden of Eden (the language we now call Hebrew), you're probably not going to believe that the same God took away the pure language of the Garden of Eden and replaced it with scores of corrupted, scrambled, and confused languages that were all obviously similar but not the same.

We begin with the premise that God created one pure language in the beginning. God compensated the wicked post flood generations by giving them the wages they had earned for the treacherous acts of sin and rebellion they demonstrated at the Tower of Babel.

God took from man the one pure language of the Garden of Eden and exchanged it for corrupted languages that sent them scurrying all over the earth with scrambled languages that allowed to man to co-alesce in accordance with the commandment the Lord gave to Noah and his sons.

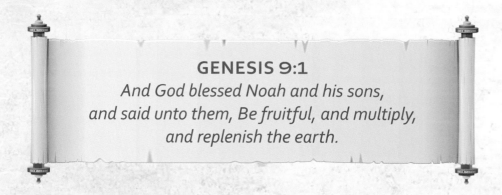

GENESIS 9:1
*And God blessed Noah and his sons,
and said unto them, Be fruitful, and multiply,
and replenish the earth.*

We can do this the easy way or the hard way!

In the end, the rebels of Babel unwillingly obeyed God's instructions to multiply and replenish the earth. The only difference was that they ended up doing so without the light of God's pure language. The LORD gave them what they wanted. The LORD gave them confused languages that would allow them to wallow in their blindness and unbelief.

The corruption of the pure language of the Garden of Eden resulted in a corruption of everything that was good. The cities and nations that developed after the flood even corrupted the creation story, giving themselves over to myths, fables, and fiction. They joined themselves to the rebellious angelic rebels and demons that had lost their preferred places in God's kingdom. They replaced worship of the only true living God with bondage to false gods and every unclean spirit that roams the earth. If they were to wallow in their blindness and unbelief, they would do so without the Lord's pure language.

GENESIS 11:8

So, the Lord scattered them abroad from thence upon the face of all the earth: and they left off to build the city.

In short, God left the "Babylonian Conspirators" answerable to their own evil imagination and devices within the boundaries of His permissive will.

What about the Language of Eden, the Language of the Garden?

God preserved His pure language, as a perpetual inheritance, to be kept unspotted and separate by a small remnant, who he would sustain forever. To the first "People of the Book" God made promises and covenants which guaranteed their survival and eventual status as a unique nation purposed with declaring His Word. By so doing, God insured the continuance of His Word in order that all men might have a witness of the Truth.

Is this why we still have the Hebrew language intact to this very day?

47

CHAPTER 6

Original Hebrew Untangles Modern Confusion

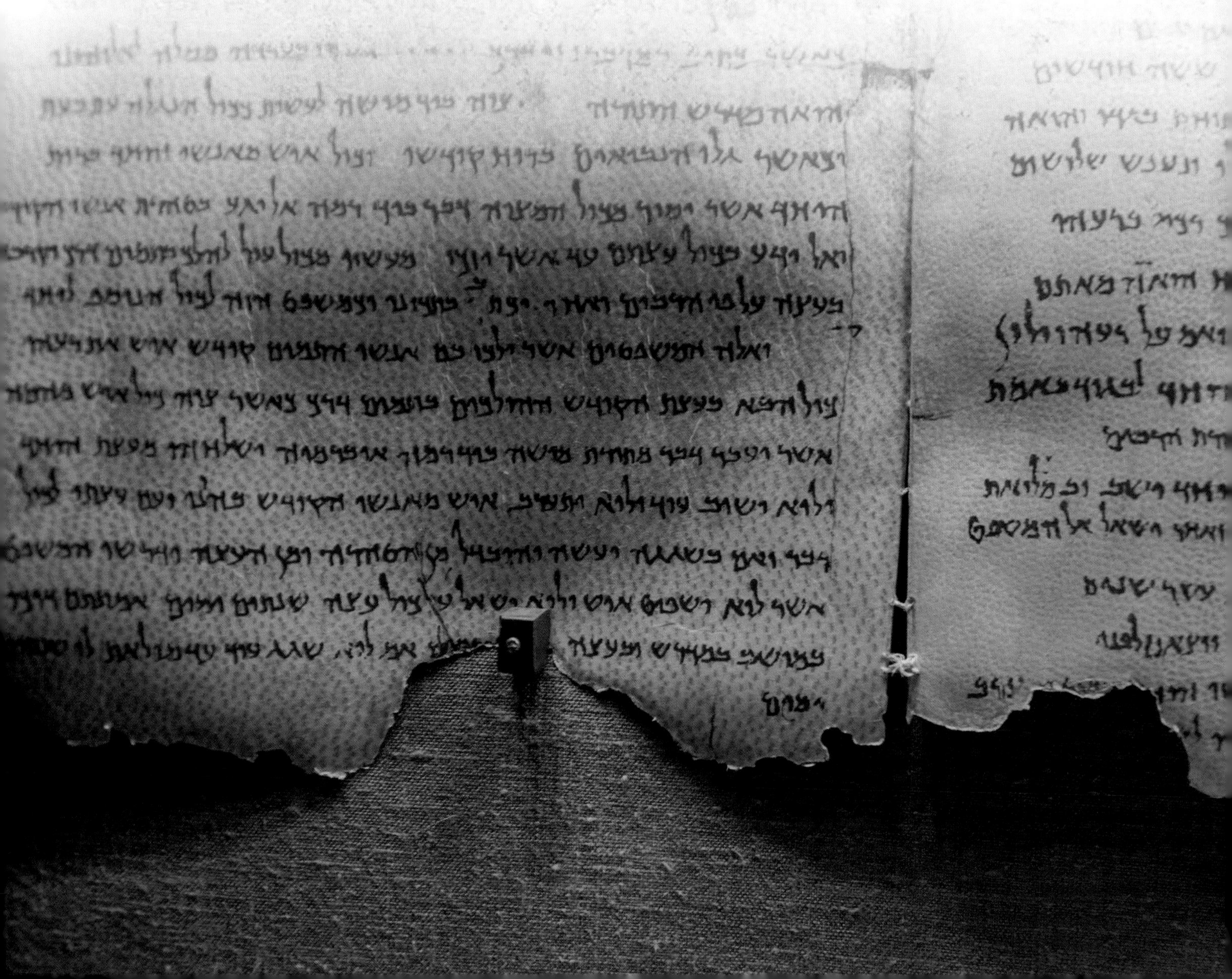

There is no confusion with the Lord God. God is not the author of confusion. And, in the end, it has no place in His kingdom.

Does God use confusion to further His gracious purposes?

We know He does.

The promise that all Christians so glibly parrot without acting like they really believe it, proves the point.

What promise is that?

ROMANS 8:28

*And we know that all things work together for good
to them that love God, to them who are the called
according to his purpose.*

The simple truth is that, while things may appear to be simply awful and headed in the wrong direction, the LORD can work it out so that it is good.

The short view of the life of Joseph is the paradoxical preamble to the end of the story of Joseph.

What was meant for evil God miraculously worked out for good.

Only God can turn something planned by His enemies to damage Him or His loved ones into something very good.

*Adding helium to a balloon does not change the balloon,
it only makes it swell up and fly high.*

Have you ever noticed how easy it is to find evidence that bolsters the ungodly opinions and theories of those that rudely mock and scoff at the very idea of a good Creator God?

Do you think this is just an unfortunate accident?

Or, does it further the purposes of God to allow those who do not love Him to find reasons to doubt His very existence?

Does God give those who hate Him the spirit of boldness in order that they might reflect outwardly and display openly what is hidden inside their minds and hearts?

We read in the English Bible that God "hardened" Pharaoh's heart. And, from that one mistranslated verse we have bolstered an entire theological viewpoint that coalesces around a complete distortion of the sovereignty of God.

Fortunately, God preserved His words, which can be read in the original Hebrew language to this day.

When we investigate the original Hebrew word translated into English as "hardened," found seven times between **Exodus 10:1** and **Exodus 14:17**, what do we find?

We discover that the Hebrew word **Chet Zayin Qoof,** the word translated as "hardened" in English is translated as "steadfast" in the original Hebrew.

We find the same Hebrew word **Chet Zayin Qoof** in **Deuteronomy 31:6.**

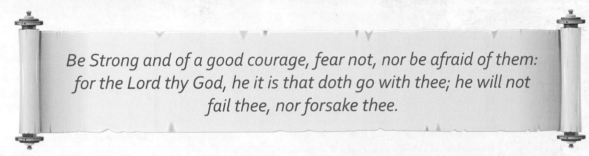

Be Strong and of a good courage, fear not, nor be afraid of them: for the Lord thy God, he it is that doth go with thee; he will not fail thee, nor forsake thee.

God did not *change* Pharaoh's heart, he simply gave Pharaoh the courage to express it without fear. Pharaoh's heart was fortified or strengthened; it was not altered or amended.

Pharaoh was given the spirit of resoluteness that resulted in him being steadfast in his convictions.

God did not harden Pharaoh's heart. Instead, He allowed what was already in Pharaoh's heart to manifest in a way that was bold and courageous.

The wickedness of Pharaoh's heart was fully revealed and displayed so that there could be no question about where Pharaoh's heart was anchored.

Pharaoh was an enemy of God, and God wanted everyone to know it.

How many times have I heard Christians wonder out loud why God didn't make the genesis of His creation undeniably and completely crystal clear as well as in harmony with all the latest scientific knowledge?

How much easier evangelism would be if there was only one creation account — the one revealed by the Creator, proven with evidence and believed by all.

Obviously, God has a better way of sorting out those that love and trust Him from those that do not.

For those who do not love God or want Him to rule over them, the Lord allowed ambivalence and blindness as a way of justifying their decisions. There is plenty of evidence that bolsters faith, but God has allowed it to co-exist with "false evidence" and easy to believe lies in order to test the heart of man.

Has an AH-HA moment arrived?

While we are musing about that question, let's reflect on why God allowed one third of the angels in Heaven to exercise their freewill by both believing and following Lucifer.

It seems to me that a simple, overwhelming glorious moment of revelation and demonstration of power would have put that entire process to a sudden and final end.

Short of Divine intervention, you might think that given the perfect context of Heaven, with all its glorious testimony to the majesty and righteousness of God, that a rebellion based on slanderous lies and skillful misrepresentations would not find a willing audience.

But it did!

What was the Lord thinking?

Is this why the Lord put one single tree in the Garden of Eden whose delicious looking fruit man as forbidden to eat?

Did God want Adam to sin?

The answer is absolutely NOT!

Adam was put in the Garden because God desired to test Adam's heart to see if he loved Him alone, or if Adam's affections lay elsewhere.

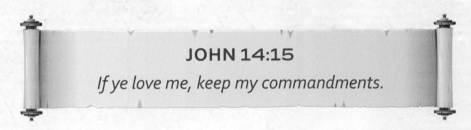

JOHN 14:15

If ye love me, keep my commandments.

God's purpose in allowing evil is not as perplexing as man imagines.

Consider an *earthly example* of a *heavenly strategy!*

If you have ever run a business large or small then at some point you may find yourself in the position of dealing with a slanderous arrogant employee who thinks he or she can do it better than you can.

You can fire that person on the spot and try to contain the damage this employee's slander has created, or you can let it run its course.

What would be the advantage of letting slanderous lies continue?

Can you figure it out?

The rebel will infect the minds of others putting their loyalty and devotion to the person signing their pay checks and providing for their families to the **TEST**!

You can guess the rest.

What better way to cleanse an organization of the "Absaloms" than to let the insurrection run its course in order to draw out the cancer of rebellion and disloyalty?

Once everyone has revealed their true hearts, then is the time to disassociate yourself from the rebels and reward the faithful, cleansing and purifying your domain.

You might even find yourself secretly allowing the rebel to make progress. Does that make you responsible for the sins of the rebel? Of course not. It simply means that you are speeding up the process of "discovery". This process of discovery will lead to the day when all will be set right again in your domain. You will be surrounded by people whose love and devotion was tested and remained faithful.

If you can see the advantages of such a strategy in an earthly enterprise, do you really think it would not have the same wonderful consequence in the kingdom of Heaven?

CHAPTER 7

Back to the Garden of Eden

Now let's go back to the topic of the one pure language that emerged unmolested from the Garden of Eden. The language that still exists today is a testimony to the miracle working power of our God and His covenant to redeem mankind through His anointed Messiah.

What does the "history of language" look like if we believe and trust God and have confidence in what He has revealed to us?

We would operate under a completely different historical timeline and perspective — the one outlined in the ancient prophetic Scriptures that we call the Old Testament.

The history of language that emerges from a "Biblical" vantage point gives us complete confidence that the language spoken by Adam and Eve, as they communicated face to face with God, is the same language God revealed in over 99% of the ancient prophetic Scriptures we know as the Old Testament.

ZEPHANIAH 3:9

For then will I turn to the people a pure language, that they may all call upon the name of the Lord, to serve him with one consent.

Prophecy is one of the ways God encourages His people to remain steadfast, courageous, and resolute!

Have you ever wondered why Satan spends so much time on false prophecy?

How many false prophets have been raised up in the service of the Dark Prince?

I would venture to guess thousands, and they keep coming.

Why?

I will answer the question with a question.

Why does the enemy of a country imitate, publish, and circulate false facsimiles of their legal currency?

The answer is simple. The abundance of counterfeit currency reduces the value and creates suspicion about the bona-fide currency.

For millennium some Bible scholars speculated and wondered what pure language God had in mind for the last days.

God has miraculously regathered His scattered chosen people from every nation on earth.

Of what "pure language" do they speak?

The re-gathering, foretold by the prophet Zephaniah, happened in 1948. We can now bear witness to the fulfillment of the prophecy of Zephaniah as it has unfolded in time as a real historical event.

I can report with 100% confidence that the pure language speculation has been solved. The language spoken in regathered Israel today is Hebrew, the same language that Adam spoke in the Garden of Eden.

It is the same language that was preserved on Noah's Ark. The same pure language preserved after God confused the languages at the Tower of Babel.

There is nothing in the Scriptures that even hints that the language spoken in the Garden of Eden was not the same language that crossed over on the ark with Noah. The language of the Garden was the same language that was spoken at the time Nimrod began building the Tower of Babel.

There were not multiple languages spoken in the pre-diluvium age, only one language was spoken.

The language spoken was the language gifted to Adam from the moment he was created.

The same can be said of the first language spoken by all the inhabitants of the newly washed earth up until the time God confused His one pure language at the Tower of Babel.

So, if you think that God confused the "pure language" during the reign of Nimrod on the earth, you are correct.

If you think that the language spoken in the Garden ceased to exist after the confusion of languages at the Tower of Babel, then you are mistaken.

The Proof Provided by Longevity

Noah, who lived to be 950 years old, and his sons and grandsons were alive and well during the era of Nimrod. They lived to see, with their own eyes, the episode recorded in the Bible under the title of The Tower of Babel.

Simple logic and the historical record, as reported in both the Holy Scriptures and the book of Jasher (referenced several times in the Old Testament and noted in the Scriptures as a reliable account of history), shows the fact that Noah and his immediate family did not participate in the building of Nimrod's tower.

Why do we not find this hard to believe?

Noah and his righteous remnant, who were present on the earth at the time of Nimrod's rebellion, did not wake up one morning speaking a foreign language. There is no evidence nor is there reason to believe that those not present, not participating, and not sanctioning the deplorable rebellion that was taking place in the Valley of Shinar ever had the Garden language removed from their hearts and minds.

There is no evidence that those NOT under the despotic and demonic rule of Nimrod ever stopped speaking the language of the Garden of Eden.

These newly confused and corrupted languages, which caused men to migrate in all directions, had their original roots in the language of the Garden of Eden. God used these corrupted languages to coalesce the people into nation groups that no longer possessed the pure revelatory purpose of the language spoken in the Garden of Eden.

Only Noah and his family retained the precious gift first given to Adam, the language of the Garden of Eden. This language was passed

on from Noah to Shem, to Eber, and finally to Abraham, Isaac, and Jacob.

Eber is where both the language and the people derive the name Hebrew. In the language of the Garden, the letter *"hey"* before a noun acts as a definite article. For example, in **Genesis 1:1** *"the heavens"* is a translation of *"h'shemayim"*. In Hebrew, *"shemayim"* simply means *"heavens"*, and when you prepend the hey, it transforms *"heavens"* to *"the heavens"*. In this same way, Abram was referred to as *"the Eber"* or *"h'ibri"* (the Hebrew).

In order to provide some historical context for this event, Abram was over 50 years old when his great grandfather Noah died. When God confused the language of rebellious men at the tower of Babel, He removed from those men the language of the Garden of Eden.

Mankind had, in less than 300 years after the flood, returned to the same pagan idolatry that brought judgment on the world in the first place.

What was the judgment God decreed upon those that participated in the rebellion of Nimod at the Tower of Babel?

The answer is that the judicial judgment of God confused their language, and God thereby removed His revelatory word from their vocabulary.

They would no longer mock God in His pure language but instead be given a language that was better suited to aid them in their quest to evict the One True God from their minds and hearts.

Notice that God could have removed all language from their hearts and minds, sending men into utter darkness that would have taken millennium to cure. But, He didn't. He left them the means to openly and loudly express the desires of their wicked hearts.

Are you starting to understand one of the revealed ways that God works?

God accommodated their rebellion, giving them over to what they desired.

God would no longer tolerate those who blasphemed Him in the pure language He had created, in order to reveal His gracious plans to mankind. If they would blaspheme and imagine vain things it would be in a confused language more suited to reflect the condition of their hearts and minds.

In short, they were sentenced to a judicial spiritual blindness.

How did that work out?

The pure language was preserved by a faithful remnant that worshiped God alone and refused to become embroiled in the rebellion of Nimrod.

Noah and his family, including Shem and Eber, did not sanction or participate in the construction of Nimrod's *star-gate* designed to breach the heavens in order to put them in contact with the ancient gods (fallen angels).

What was the ultimate goal of Nimrod's tower?

Do not be confused. Babel was constructed in the Plains of Shinar in order to crash the gates of Heaven, invade God's kingdom, and destroy the Creator God.

CHAPTER 8

Hebrew the Original or a Sloppy Copy?

Now let's take a look at the ancient languages of the pagan nations of Sumerian, Phoenicia, Egypt, and China.

They all began as pictographic languages full of iconic symbols that became objects of worship.

Over the ages, archeologists have unearthed many of the clay and stone mediums that display the symbols used in pagan languages. These languages sprang up without any evolutionary history.

Fallen men now communicating in a corrupted language will no doubt continue the process of corruption.

Evidence of this is not surprising. But, what is perplexing, to those that study ancient languages, is the absence of the long ages of development required by the theories that undergird modern linguistic theory.

These "corrupted" languages literally sprang up out of nowhere.

Consider the millions of intermediate skeletal remains that must be present to support the theory of evolution.

Where are they?

They simply do not exist!

All the evidence, when honestly investigated, is consistent with the Biblical record that documents the account found in the **11th chapter of Genesis.**

To be clear, there is no history or evidence of the long march of language from primitive to advanced.

Like Darwin's missing intermediary fossils, which must be present to bear witness to an evolution of a species, the same missing data is evidence that there was NO evolution of language.

Obviously, there were changes over time to accommodate modernity, but there is no evidence of the process that would have taken thousands of years to unfold with tons of evidence of how it all developed.

The pathway from mute to *master of ceremony* simply does not exist.

The language of Paganism and Humanism

Now, consider the symbols or pictograms that composed the post Babel languages, that we are told were the precursors to Hebrew.

See if you can notice a pattern.

The ancient pictographic languages of the Phoenicians, Egyptians, Sumerians, Akkadians, Chinese, and all additional post-diluvium languages, which sprang up after the Tower of Bable, show the sun, moon, and stars dipected as sacred entities and objects of worship.

Man's technology, if indeed it was originated with man, is lifted up in these pagan pictographic languages that were birthed in the chaos, confusion, and pride that followed Babel.

You might think that humanism and paganism are mutually exclusive. Think again!

They regularly show up together as they are two sides to the same coin. "Enlightened" paganism is the twin brother of the priests of so-called science and technology.

When you look at the Egyptian, Sumerian, and Chinese pictograms what do you notice?

	EGYPTIAN	SUMERIAN	CHINESE
BOATS			船
CARTS PULLED BY OXEN, MULES, AND HORSES			车

Notice the following weapons:

	EGYPTIAN	SUMERIAN	CHINESE
SPEARS			枪
BOWS AND ARROWS			張
SLINGS			纠
SWORDS			刀
WHIPS			纠

	EGYPTIAN	SUMERIAN	CHINESE
BODY ARMOR			铁
CHARIOTS			兵

Notice the adornment and sensualizing of women:

	EGYPTIAN	SUMERIAN	CHINESE
JEWELRY			
BODILY ADORNMENTS AND VESTMENTS			
MAKE-UP			

Notice the division of classes of men from the lowliest to the most elevated:

	EGYPTIAN	SUMERIAN	CHINESE
SLAVES IN BONDAGE			奴
CATTLE IN BONDAGE			牛
CONQUERED ARMIES			胜利军

	EGYPTIAN	SUMERIAN	CHINESE
LABORERS			劳动
SERVANTS			奴仆

Notice the elevation of man's technology as evidenced by the architecture displayed in and on the "sacred" monuments of the post-Babel societies:

	EGYPTIAN	SUMERIAN	CHINESE
CHARIOTS			
WAGONS			
SHRINES			
TEMPLES			
MAUSOLEUMS			
PALACES			

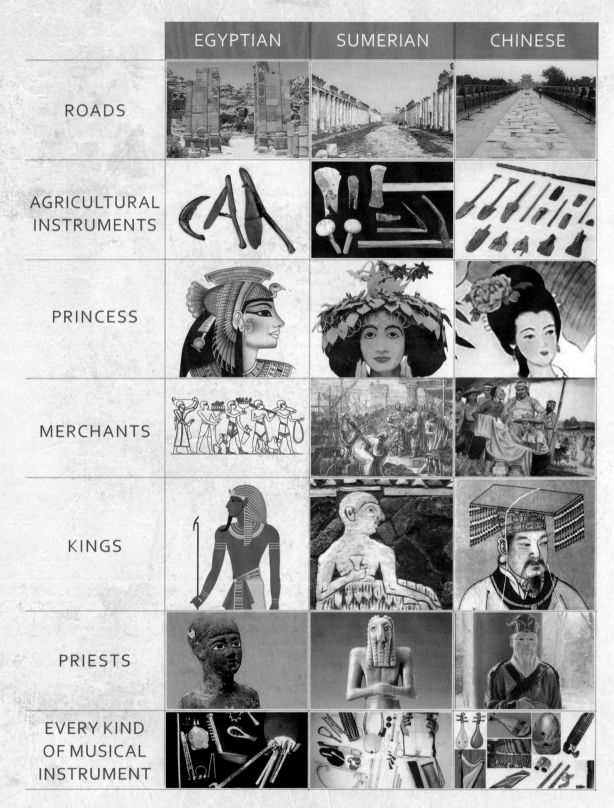

	EGYPTIAN	SUMERIAN	CHINESE
ROADS			
AGRICULTURAL INSTRUMENTS			
PRINCESS			
MERCHANTS			
KINGS			
PRIESTS			
EVERY KIND OF MUSICAL INSTRUMENT			

VS
The Language of Redemption
There is a lot to be said by Silence!

Compare all the above to the simple pictures that undergird the Hebrew language, the language of the Garden of Eden.

Consider the 22 pictograms of the Ox, Tent, Camel, Door, Man Lifting Up his Hands, to Look, Nail or Stake, Harvesting Tool, Garden, Sanctuary, Snake, Arm, Hand, Staff, Water, Fish or Sprout, Prop for Tree, Eye, Mouth, Hook, Back of Head, Head Person, Teeth, Wooden Cross.

Now notice what you don't see in the language of the Garden of Eden.

You do not see pictographs of wheels, spears, or arrows.

There are no ox carts, no boats, no jewelry, no slavery, no whips, no beasts of burden, no sun, no moon, no stars to worship, no palaces, no monuments to death, no graven idols, no cities, no musical instruments, no metal works, no sword play, no warfare, no chariots of war drawn by horses, no infantry, and no works of man are pictured in any of the 22 pictures that undergird the 22 letters in the Hebrew alphabet.

The simple truth is that there is not one single picture in the palate of 22 pictures that is not consistent with life in the Garden of Eden before the fall.

Adam is not the man you think he is!

Let's return to Adam and the Garden of Eden in order to get our compass pointing in the right direction.

Our understanding and imagination need to be disabused of any preconceived image of Adam as a knuckle dragging primitive man.

Adam understood a lot more than any of us can ever imagine.

Do you have a copy machine?

Have you ever made a copy from an original?

The first copy can be pretty good.

If you continue to make copies using the last copy as your new original, it will not be long before you end up with a copy that is a very poor distorted reflection of the original image you copied.

Comparing the original with a 10th generation copy illustrates the point I am trying to make.

Adam was created sinless. His capacities in his un-fallen state were far superior to anything we can now imagine. His intellectual capacity must have been off the charts.

The question has been asked, could Adam read and write?

The question assumes that if he could not, then he was both primitive and ignorant.

This very question does not discover ignorance — it displays ignorance.

You cannot even imagine the capacities of the first created man whose life, even after cut off from the life support of God's Spirit, took 930 days to shrivel up and finally expire.

Can you compare that to any modern examples?

Adam, if alive today, would be considered more than a freak of nature. He would be considered a little god.

Even though that description is an affront to the Creator, it would be the "natural" response of fallen man to view Adam as a superman with "godlike" capacities. There was only one first man, and He was created both sinless and with unimaginable abilities that we are simply unable to comprehend.

So, why exactly would Adam, with abilities and a memory that would put any supercomputer manufactured by modern man to shame, need to read or write?

Perhaps, Adam did know how to write.

With his ability to retain information and understand all the nuances of the language, the question is — why would Adam need to write?

Adam did not have a faulty memory. He did not need to take notes in order to ponder the mysteries Elohim revealed to him during his tenure in the Garden of Eden.

God has plans for the future!

Here is where we come face to face with the miracle of God's pure language.

By the Creator's design, from the beginning, the language of the Garden perfectly accomplished its purpose before and after the fall of Adam.

It was a language that could easily be written down and understood.

The language of the Garden of Eden contained, from the beginning, the redemptive purpose that YHVH Elohim (the LORD God) had for man after his expulsion from the Garden of Eden.

It was a language that anticipated the fall of man without having to change a single letter, picture, or number.

I know what you're thinking.

Obviously, words that were unfamiliar to Adam in the Garden of Eden would be constructed from the letters in the Hebrew alphabet in order that men might communicate in this newly fallen and changing sinful world.

Some pictures and concepts were widened in order to accommodate the new reality of man's sin. The rebellion of Adam would no doubt be reflected in the language that came out of the Garden.

The most seemingly incongruous example is the seventh Hebrew Symbol in the Hebrew Aleph-Beyt.

The meaning of the Number 7 and the Axe

ZAYIN
7

Let's consider for a moment the Hebrew letter Zayin which was originally pictured as an axe and could probably serve the dual purpose as a hammer.

I have chosen this letter since it is the one symbol that is most often questioned.

The modern Hebrew letter Zayin is viewed as a symbol for a knife or sword weapon.

ZAYIN

The weapon does not seem to be in harmony with the original symbol revealed in the Garden of Eden.

Adam did not need a sword to defend himself as there was nothing hostile living within the confines of the Garden.

So, what is this all about?

The answer to the meaning of Zayin is discovered in the number seven.

There are only nine numbers in the world, as zero is not a number but a place holder.

Of all nine numbers, there are four numbers that are considered sacred. These numbers are constantly used in the Bible as a shadow of something divine and sacred.

3

The number **Three**, for example, is the sacred number that means **Divine Perfection**.

10

Ten is the number that means **Ordinal Perfection**. Ordinal Perfection simply means that something ordained in Heaven has unfolded or is unfolding on the earth. Ten is the one number that notifies us that God has plans for mankind.

12

Based on its usage in Scripture, we see that the number **Twelve** is the number of **Governmental Perfection**. It is the one number that is associated with God's Kingdom and the fact that one day it will be the kingdom of this world.

Isn't this what the Lord told us to pray for?

His kingdom has not arrived yet, and so we continue to pray, "May Thy Kingdom Come".

The fourth sacred number is **Seven**. Seven is used throughout the Scriptures to reveal **Devine Completion**.

So, what does all of this have to do with an axe and the number seven?

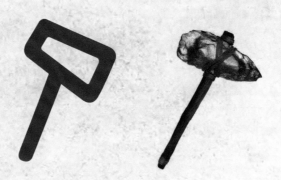

The Lesson of the Fruit Tree

Of all the tools Adam would need as the caretaker of the Garden of Eden an axe would have been the most necessary and useful.

Trees need pruning, young saplings would need to be secured to a stake with vine ropes, and fruit needs harvesting. The list could go on and on.

When harvest time arrived, the axe made from a sharp shale stone attached to a handle made from a sturdy stick and fastened by a vine rope would have been an important harvesting tool.

A sharp axe would have been used for harvesting or "cutting off" the fully ripened fruit.

If you think that all fruit is simply pulled or shaken off a fruit tree then you are probably unaware of the fact that most fruit is actually "cut" off the tree or vine. All grapes are harvested with a pruning knife. Many varieties of fruit would be damaged if they were pulled off the fruit tree, so are either clipped or cut from the tree.

When are things harvested?

The answer is when they are fully ripened. The harvest begins at exactly the right time. If you leave the fruit on the trees past the point when God designed them to be harvested what is the result?

The fruit attached to the tree would simply rot and fall off the tree where it would decay.

There is a time to harvest.

When is that time?

When the trees function of producing fruit is complete.

Do you see the principle of Divine Completion and the number seven at work?

Consider how many biblical truths are illustrated in the context of harvesting fruit. The axe was the original symbol of harvest time, the time of completion.

When is an Axe not a Harvesting Tool?

Zayin is pictured in modern Hebrew script as a knife or a sword. In short, Zayin is pictured as not only a harvesting tool but also a weapon.

ZAYIN in modern Hebrew Script

It is not hard to imagine an Axe or Hammer being used as a weapon.

The axe was not a weapon in the Garden of Eden.

Consider how the meaning of Zayin expanded after Adam was expelled from the Garden.

The connection between being "Cut Off" and Completion!

Consider the first fruits of *sin:*

What does this have to do with Zayin?

Was something "cut off"?

The answer is *yes.*

The life of Abel was "cut off" by the violent act of his brother Cain.

Sin changed everything, except the language of the Garden of Eden.

God knew what was going to happen after the perfection of the Garden of Eden, and He architected His language so that it would be a light of revelation in a world darkened by the new reality of sin.

Did the fact that the axe went from being used as a harvesting tool to a weapon diminish the word of God?

No, it magnified it.

Only God could have known that the picture he gave Adam for the seventh letter of the Aleph-Beyt would one day have spiritual significance as it related to both the harvesting of fruit and the end times final harvest of the souls of men — a time that comes to a violent and finally a peaceful conclusion as *sin* is finally "cut off" and discarded forever and ever.

We are told that Jesus was "cut off". This was not a mistake, it was an accomplishment that is associated with Zayin and the number seven. It may be hard to fully grasp the truth of the matter, but when Jesus spoke those final words from the cross of Calvary, "It is finished.", He was announcing Divine Completion.

Consider the above as you review the meaning of the picture and number embedded in the seventh letter in the Hebrew Aleph-Beyt.

HARVEST

7 ZAYIN

Completeness – Resurrection – To Be Full – To Be Satisfied –
Perfect – The Seventh Day that is a
Prophetic Harbinger of the Millennial Reign of Christ –
Eternal Sabbath and Everlasting Perfection –
God the Father's Perfection – Inspiration of the Holy Spirit

DIVINE COMPLETION

CHAPTER 9

The Language of Omniscience

Contact with the Hebrew language brings you in contact with the Omniscient Creator!

Consider the omniscient foresight that went into designing the language of the perfect Garden of Eden in such a way that its full force and miraculous prophetic power was only fully manifest after sin entered the world.

Why is this?

The answer should be plain. God created a language that made the seemingly impossible transition from a sinless Garden to a sinful world of thorns and thistles, without losing but rather highlighting His original purpose.

What was that original purpose?

The answer can be found in one word.

The word is the revelation of Messiah.

The Hebrew language is designed at its very root to communicate the message of Messianic atonement and redemption.

What we know as phonetic or conventional Hebrew was ordained by God to be the primary means of communicating His revelation to fallen mankind.

Without this gracious revelation where would we be?

I shudder to think!

That does not change the way God architected the language from the beginning — three complimentary languages disclosing one revelation.

Three-in-One, where have we heard that before?

Are the pictures and numbers the cheering section
for the conventional Hebrew text?

The *number language* relies on the *conventional language* primarily but also on the *picture language* to give it meaning. Without the conventional Hebrew language, the numbers represented by each letter and the combination of letter/numbers would have no meaning, as their context is tied to both the pictures and the phonetic Hebrew.

At this point I need to clear up some confusion.

The language of the Garden, what we call Hebrew, was originally a 22-letter language that was written with no punctuation, no spaces between the letters, and no phonetic notations.

Each letter, or pictogram, was also two numbers.

One number is called the *place number,* and it is simply the number associated with the placement or position of each of the 22 pictograms in the Aleph-Beyt.

So, Aleph the first letter was number one. And, Tav the last letter was number 22.

The second number connected to each of the 22 letters compose a mathematical system that is pictured below in the early Hebrew pictograms. This number is called the *value number,* as it is the number God associated with each individual one of the 22 Hebrew letters.

Remember that Hebrew is read from right to left.

Early Hebrew Pictograms (Script) Pre-Babylonian Captivity
(Hebrew that Abraham, Moses, David, and the Prophets could read.)

CHET	ZAYIN	VAV	HEY	DALET	GIMEL	BEYT	ALEPH
8	7	6	5	4	3	2	1
NUMBER POSITION							
8	7	6	5	4	3	2	1
VALUE NUMBER							

AYIN	SAMECH	NOON	MEM	LAMED	KAF	YOOD	TET
16	15	14	13	12	11	10	9
NUMBER POSITION							
70	60	50	40	30	20	10	9
VALUE NUMBER							

TAV	SHEEN	REYSH	QOOF	TSADE	PEY
22	21	20	19	18	17
NUMBER POSITION					
400	300	200	100	90	80
VALUE NUMBER					

Babylonian Exile results in the modification of the Hebrew Symbols

The following five Hebrew letters were altered, repeated, and then added to the Hebrew Aleph-Beyt during the Babylonian exile around 500 years BC. The five letters that were duplicated were given a numerical value number that does not correspond to the value number of the original early Hebrew.

The following alterations were made to the modern Hebrew block script.

These extra five variations on the already existing five letters are called "sofit" letters and are used when they occur at the end of a Hebrew word.

The five sofit letters with their new designated number are as follows:

Kaf = 500, **Mem** = 600, **Noon** = 700

Pey = 800 **Tsade** = 900

For example:

ב Kaf is originally the number 20

The altered form of ך Kaf, used only at the end of a word based on modern Hebrew block script has now been associated with the number 500.

מ Mem is the number 40

The altered form of ם Mem, used only at the end of a word based on modern Hebrew block script, is now the number 600.

נ Noon is the number 50

The altered form of ן Noon, used only at the end of a word based on modern Hebrew block script, is now the number 700.

פ Pey is the number 80

The altered form of ף Pey, used only at the end of a word based on modern Hebrew block script, is now the number 800.

צ Tsade is the number 90

The altered form of ץ Tsade, used only at the end of a word based on modern Hebrew block script, is now the number 900.

The addition of the five new variations of the already existing five Hebrew letters indicate the end of a Hebrew word.

These five new additions have also been introduced to increase the top end of the numeric system from 400 to 900.

Man thinks he can do better!

Left to the capricious schemes of man, we would all probably have multiple appendages and two sets of eyes so that we could walk in two directions at once while seeing both forwards and backwards.

Change after all is a good thing!

Right?

Consider the changes made to the Hebrew Aleph-Beyt while Judah was in captivity in Babylon.

Think of how it expanded the numbers and modified the pictures in such a way that they no longer were easily identifiable.

Are these good ideas?

They certainly must have thought so at the time, after all, who needs all these child-like pictograms as we are all grown-ups now? Can you hear the words of Jesus ringing in your ears?

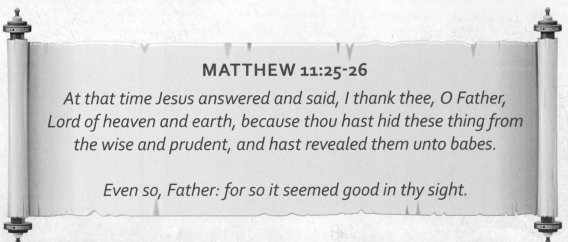

MATTHEW 11:25-26

At that time Jesus answered and said, I thank thee, O Father, Lord of heaven and earth, because thou hast hid these thing from the wise and prudent, and hast revealed them unto babes.

Even so, Father: for so it seemed good in thy sight.

None of these changes, which took place during the Babylonian captivity, have any Scriptural warrant, as they were not part of the original revelation from God.

This book will display the early Hebrew symbols and numbers, based on God's original disclosure, in addition to the modern Hebrew script that everyone is familiar with.

Mem is the picture of water and originally the number 40. Mem does not change to the number 600 just because some unnamed scribe, who had been banished to Babylon because of unbelief, decided to present it as a variation of the other altered letter Mem in order to give it a new numeric meaning when it comes at the end of a Hebrew word.

We have accommodated ourselves to the modern block Hebrew, since that is what everyone is familiar with.

We see no reason to change the number designation based on the changes made during the Babylonian captivity, which took place approximately 500 years before the birth of Jesus.

To keep things simple, we have decided to always include the earliest pictographic symbols.

These are the early symbols that were revealed to Moses by God — symbols all Israel could read.

Moses would be unable to read modern Hebrew without re-learning all the symbols since most bear little or no resemblance to the pictures they originally represent.

To be fair, there are a couple notable exceptions — proof positive that the Holy Spirit was present in Babylon making sure that the changes made in the pure language did not go beyond certain sovereignly ordained boundaries.

The picture and number translations used in the book are based on the earliest Hebrew pictograms and numbers. These are not only the most authentic and ancient, but they also clearly display the supernatural significance of the language gifted to Adam and preserved to this day.

Most Christians believe that the conventional Hebrew language stands alone as the single witness of God's revelation to mankind, as recorded in the anciet prophetic text we call the Old Testament.

Truly, the ancient prophetic, phonetic, and written text does *stand*. It does not stand alone as it was embedded from the beginning with prophetic pictures and numbers.

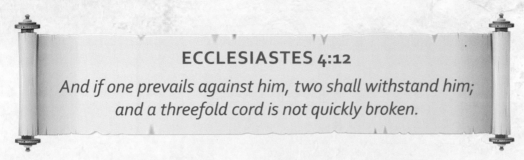

ECCLESIASTES 4:12

*And if one prevails against him, two shall withstand him;
and a threefold cord is not quickly broken.*

God has incredible ways of getting into our imagination!

There is nothing more lucid than the biblical narrative revealed with the visual aids of pictures and numbers.

Pictures and numbers that were retained in a form that represented something man was familiar with — objects and symbols that would always be understood and would not change.

Obviously, carving a symbol into stone can be accomplished with the greatest ease by producing angular symbols. Using a stylus to press symbols into wet clay will allow for a more artistic representation. Penning it on parchment opens up yet another avenue of expression.

God did not give Adam a set of 22 flash cards with a prescribed picture that must be traced with exactitude. Rather, God put a picture into Adam's mind. It was a picture that could easily be understood and traced out in order to be easily figured out by all that viewed it.

These symbols were not designed by God to be difficult to decipher, just the opposite is true. A child could easily figure them out. The Hebrew language was not revealed to hide a secret. It was revealed to disclose everlasting *truth,* as its prophetic harbingers unfolded for all mankind to witness.

God was the one who linked the picture to a number. This was not only useful to Adam, whose intelligence was not challenged by the difficulty of sorting out the meaning of both pictures and numbers at the same time. The pictures and numbers are also useful in the *"here and now"* as they are laden with theological and prophetic meaning.

Are we surprised that the spiritual significance of numbers and the child-like revelation of pictures has been hidden, corrupted, and finally packaged by those that hate God and His Son in a way that makes it toxic for Christians?

How many times have I heard that any attempt to understand the spiritual significance of numbers in Scripture is unwarranted, the devil's playground, and workshop for the Kabbalist and similar cults?

There are now at least two prominent enemies of truth, two liars.

Satan has raised up a legion of false priests who have corrupted the pictures and numbers originally revealed in the ancient prophetic text we call the Old Testament.

There is a second class of liars who claim to be defenders of the truth when in fact they are puffed up speed bumps who wish to defend people from the truth.

These self-appointed Bible police, without warrant or reason, accuse anyone that investigates numbers in Scripture of cooperating with the *"dark side"*.

I don't know which lie is worse as they are both designed by the father of lies to prevent Christians from coming into contact with the spiritual significance of God's numbers as used in the Holy Scriptures.

This is not to say that there are not those that misuse the numbers and pictures of Scriptures, just as there are those that misuse the conventional text.

Do we ban the conventional text because there may be some who misuse it?

That has been tried in the past by those with a religious spirit and the results are evidenced by the sad and violent history that was emblematic of this devilish enterprise. Those who put themselves in charge of *"dispensing"* the truth themselves became complicit in mishandling, misinterpreting, and manipulating the Word of God.

CHAPTER 10

Investigating the First Letter in the Bible: Beyt

We will now begin giving the reader the foundational truths that will unseal the prophetic meaning of the words revealed in the Bible.

It would be logical to start with the first word in the Bible. The first and most amazing prophetic disclosure in the Bible. A prophetic disclosure that sweeps across the history of man, pinpointing for our enlightenment the most significant events that have ever happened or will happen in human history.

And, that is where I began, only to discover that the amazing revelation found in the first six pictographs were a repository for such a wealth of information that the few paragraphs I had planned to unveil its meaning were not enough. It turned out a chapter was not enough. Months later, an entire book, that really only scratched the surface, was finally produced.

That book is now available to the reader. It is titled **THE BERISHEET PASSOVER PROPHECY – The End Revealed by God in the Beginning**.

Berisheet "In Beginning"

The rest of this book is written for those that want to know what was on God's mind when He first revealed the language of the Garden of Eden. Once you have finished reading this book, we strongly recommend that you avail yourself to **The Berisheet Passover Prophecy.**

You will find this book in the library of **RockIslandBooks.com**.

Now, to begin a fruitful and insightful journey that will leave you filled with hope for the future and a love for the only One who holds the future in His hands. A future that was designed by God to work together for all those that love God, in order that in the end you will discover His goodness directed toward you.

The following is a brief overview of the first letter in the first word in the Bible. Keep in mind that this is just a few bread crumbs. A feast awaits those who investigate this amazing work. You can discover much more in The Berisheet Passover Prophecy.

The First Letter in the First Word of the First Book in the Bible

Let's look at the very first script or letter in the Bible. The letter Beyt, the second letter in the 22 letter Hebrew Aleph-Beyt.

This single solitary letter should clue us into the fact that God knows the deepest longings and desires of man's heart.

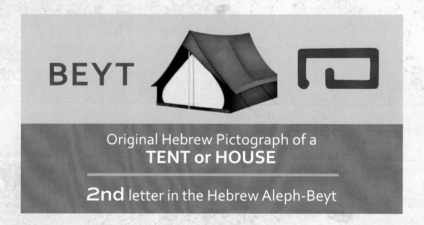

BEYT

Original Hebrew Pictograph of a
TENT or HOUSE

2nd letter in the Hebrew Aleph-Beyt

House – Tent – Son – Family – Dwelling Place –
The Physical Tent/Body – Inside – Within
First letter in the Torah that identifies the Son of God

Beyt, the first letter in the Bible, means *in or inside* and is pictured as the floor plan for a tent or a house.

In other words, God introduces Himself to spiritually homeless man as the Creator of the Home that man has carelessly abandoned and is prevented, in his present sinful state, from ever entering.

Mankind is Spiritually Homeless

Home is not presented by God as a taunt but a hope.

Isn't that consistent with what we know about the loving heart of our Heavenly Father?

God reserves the place of honor and prominence in the very first letter that He introduces to us. It is the subplot of all that follows.

It is all about *home!*

If you want proof that God knows the interior of men's hearts then here it is in one single word, **HOME**.

The deepest longing in the heart of man is to be at *home!*

Sinner Come Home!

By the time you have finished meditating on the first six letters in the first word in the Bible, you can add two more words in front of *home.*

Do you know what they are?

Come!
Come home!

Finally, you can add a third word.

Sinner!
Sinner come home!

But how is this possible?

The first word in the Bible readily and without manipulation or persuasion gives up the answer as it gives us the unambiguous picture of the Son of God joined inexplicably to the mystery of the wooden cross!

What do we discover when we read the carefully preserved pictures and consider the numbers revealed in God's love letter to mankind?

What is it that weighs heavy on our Heavenly Father's heart, a heart filled with love and mercy?

Amazingly, God has made it possible for us to discover what is on His mind.

In fact, He wants us to know!

Do you care to look?

What will we find?

Prompted by a divine impulse or simple curiosity, what will we discover everywhere in His Word?

It all begins with one single word, one divine word.

Is it truly a love letter as Christians claim?

What will we discover?

Something precious or something perilous?

What is the One Big Idea of Scripture?

While it is true that we discover an unflattering portrait of our sinful and sorrowful state, we also discover His gracious plans and purpose for mankind.

Is that the centerpiece of God's revelation?

Or, is it a prelude to something much more amazing?

If we read His revelation and do not recognize ourselves as a sinful and hopeless descendant of the first sinner Adam, then we are blind to the clear revelations contained in the Scripture.

Certainly, we will be touched by His promise of home.

But is there something even greater in view?

The answer is yes!

What is it?

It is God's own Son!

Pattern is Prophecy!

God has incredible ways of getting into our imagination.

He might even draw His precious little children a picture or perhaps even 22 pictures. He might embolden each picture with a number. He might then use those pictures and numbers in His Word in order to reveal just exactly how He intends to love us.

He might, and He did!

How did God love us?

Let's answer this question by providing two pictures — one from the Old Testament and the other from the New Testament.

If you doubt the significance and efficacy of pictographic revelation then you need to consider this simple illustration of the power of a picture.

We find the mysterious picture in the conventional Hebrew text followed by the revelation of the meaning of the picture by the very one whose shadow was lifted up on a wooden stake.

Shadow

NUMBERS 21:8

And the Lord said unto Moses, Make thee a fiery serpent, and set it upon a pole: and it shall come to pass, that every one that is bitten, when he looketh upon it, shall live.

Now Listen to what Jesus said.

Reality

JOHN 3:14-15

And as Moses lifted up the serpent in the wilderness, even so must the Son of man be lifted up:

That whosoever believeth in him should not perish, but have eternal life.

Get the Picture?

CHAPTER 11

History of Hebrew Language

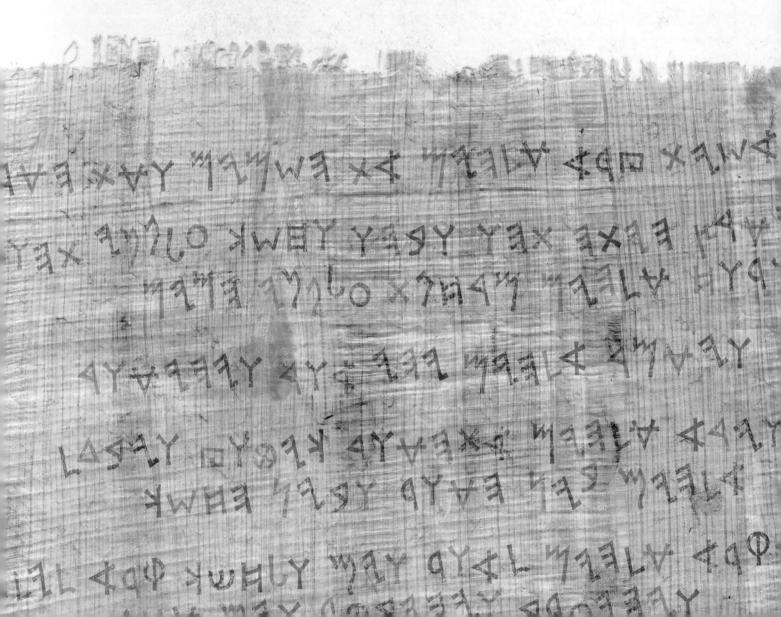

Let's take a look at this from the beginning.

As we have previously established, Abram was the first person in the Bible to be called a Hebrew. A reference to Eber, the grandson of Noah, is cited in extra-biblical history as an antagonist of Nimrod. He was an outspoken opponent of the tyranny and seditious plots that were the foundational impetus for the building of the Tower of Babel.

Abraham is directly connected to the language Noah preserved as a living breathing testimony that the language of Eden remained the one gift God allowed fallen man to retain.

God did not begin to build His *"holy nation"* until Abraham was 100 years old. This would have been around 2000 years from creation and 400 years after the flood of Noah.

During that post-flood period, great nations sprung up all with different languages?

So, are we to be intimidated by the fact that the landscape is littered with pictographic languages that all were variations of the one language.

God did not eliminate the one language, the language of the Garden. He confused it. He jumbled it up so that it lost its supernatural revelatory majesty and power.

Are we to imagine that God confused the language of righteous Noah and the remnant seed of Shem, which included Abram?

Of course not.

Was there a nation called *Noah-Ville,* a large competing nation, alongside the Sumerians, Akkadians, Egyptians, Chinese and Phoenicians?

NO!

Noah and those in his family remembered the judgment of the flood.

Noah and his family retained the memory of God's grace.

Noah and his family remained faithful to the Lord.

Remember, it was a tiny remnant, who retained their knowledge and belief in God and His Word. This small group of men did not become a nation until God decided to make them His special people.

The Hebrews entered Egypt as a small seemingly insignificant family. *Four hundred years* later, they exited Egypt as a nation.

It was 400+ years from when God made the promise to Abraham that He would make of him a great nation.

That nation began with one miracle child named Isaac *"Laughter"*, who was born when Abraham was 100 years old.

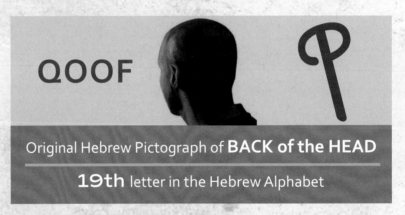

QOOF

Original Hebrew Pictograph of **BACK of the HEAD**

19th letter in the Hebrew Alphabet

Qoof means – Behind – The Last – The Least

QOOF 100

God's Promise to Children of Israel
Election – Children of The Promise

The number 100 is the letter Qoof. Qoof, the number 100, is also the picture of the *least.* Qoof is the one picture and number that identifies the Children of Promise.

After nearly half a millennium, God fulfilled His promise to Abraham. Isaac, the miracle child of promise, was born when Abraham was 100 years old. He would become the offspring of a chosen people, a nation that would be forever connected to the promises of God.

Are you beginning to get the picture?

Unearthing evidence of a language that resembled Hebrew after the flood and after the tower of Babel but before God promised Abram that he would be the father of a great nation, which would bring forth the Messiah, should not be a test of our faith.

It is obvious to anyone who simply believes the Bible and the biblical account as literal history. All that is left is to apply a little common sense.

God's Word is eternal and never changing. We are assured by the only one who cannot lie that His Word will endure forever!

Jesus reminded Satan, the great accuser and deceiver, that *"Man does not live by bread alone but by every word that proceeds from the mouth of God."*

What Word?

Was it the Word that God gifted Adam?

Was it the Word that was spoken without tutoring?

Was it the Word that did not evolve on the earth nor spring forth from sinful corrupted languages that followed in the wake of the judgment of Babel?

Was it the Word that was created fully formed in the heart, soul, and mind of the first man, which was preserved for all eternity and the only language God calls the pure language?

If you imagine that God allowed His Word, the Living Word that would miraculously be clothed with human flesh in order to save fallen mankind, to be birthed by the cursed and corrupted languages that were vomited out of the Tower of Babel then you need to rethink your understanding and bring it in line with revealed truth.

God has already supplied ample apologetic standards by which this matter can be judged.

Consider that nothing takes the Lord by surprise. So, we should not be surprised that His language is *self-authenticating,* set apart, and supernaturally transmitted in an instant to Adam. Finally, His language cannot be imitated.

How is that possible you might ask?

The next chapter will give you the answer.

The Self-Authenticating Miracle Language of the Garden of Eden

Consider how the Hebrew "letters" are so closely identified with the picture and number that God originally linked to the script. In most cases, the name of the "letter" is also the very word that identifies the picture, and in the remaining cases the root words make it clear what is in view.

The Assault on God's Word

The greatest change made to the original language of the Garden of Eden took place in, of all places, Babylon. Not at the Tower of Babel where God Himself confused the languages while at the same time preserving the one pure language of the Garden of Eden.

The first real change to the Hebrew language happened in Babylon, approximately 500 years before the birth of Jesus. The irony of this should not be lost.

The original pictographs that had endured for over 3400 years were stylistically changed to conform to the block Babylonian language we call Aramaic.

The original pictograms have not been lost. They exist and have been preserved in stone, in clay, and on parchment.

The assault that drastically refashioned the letters took place while Judah was in exile in Babylon, where God gave them over to their idolatrous passions.

Think about that for a moment!

But, the essence, the breath of God captured in the pictures and numbers could not be defaced. And, never will be, not even in the jaws of Babylon.

God will preserve His Word forever.

If it were not true you would not be reading this book.

To be clear, Enoch, Noah, Abraham, Jacob, Moses, David, and most of the prophets—save perhaps Daniel and the minor prophets—would not be able to read modern Hebrew.

Think about that for a moment.

No one but God could have ordained, from the beginning, a means of communicating His purpose and the divine portrait of His precious only begotten Son in a way that defied corruption, revealed God's unchanging plan to redeem mankind and yet was so simple to read that a child could understand it.

The Garden language we now call the Hebrew language is permanently bonded to the pictures and numbers that undergird it in order to memorialize forever the portrait and mission of His only begotten Son.

If you are a child of God, supernaturally indwelt by the Spirit of Truth that Yeshua promised would be the surety of every one of His precious flock, then you will hear His voice and follow Him.

You can hardly investigate a single Hebrew word, letter by letter, in the original pictographic script without the Son of God contemporizing Himself.

If you want a daily encounter with the Son of God, then read His Word daily. And, as you feast on the Words of Life you might consider adding in a Hebrew word study based on the pictures and numbers.

Open up your Hebrew Interlinear and find a Hebrew word that touches your heart. Take each letter and see what emerges from one single word when you investigate the pictures that compose the Hebrew word. Pray for direction from God's Spirit, just like you do when you read your English translation of His precious Word.

Keep in mind that God has preserved His written Word, and this should be the anchor-point for any investigation. If any interpretation appears to change or disagree with the conventional meaning of any word (vs. amplifying it), it requires more prayer and seeking.

The portrait that unfolds will very often pull your heart heavenward, alerting you to the fact that God's Word is living and active.

The Hebrew pictures and numbers do not contain another Gospel.

God forbid!

Anyone who misuses the original pictures and numbers to create confusion is under the same curse as anyone who dishonestly commends false doctrine based on the phonetic Hebrew language. The pictures and numbers simply amplify and magnify the already abundant and generous revelation that God has given to anyone who reads His revelation in the plain text.

There is no battle between the conventional Hebrew revelation and the revelation in the pictures and numbers.

Have you ever read an amplified New Testament?

It is a wonderful experience to consider all the linguistic nuances that are missing in the English Bible that are revealed in an amplified version of the New Testament. It is faith building and instructive. *(We recommend Kenneth Wuest).*

In much the same way, the word studies based on the original Hebrew pictures and numbers are simply a way of digging out nuances that you might just pass over without giving it any thought.

As a kid I loved to water ski.

I never had it in my mind to criticize scuba divers.

One sails over the surface, and what a joy that is.

The other plumbs the depths to discover things that are passed over quickly with no notice.

Water skiing and scuba diving are not at odds with one another.

They are both means of enjoying and investigating the same body of water, and there need be no quarrel between them.

Those who raise a controversy over the matter of Hebrew being pictographic are simply ignorant of the topic at hand or have some other agenda to push.

It is true that you can be aware of the conventional Hebrew language with no knowledge of the pictures and numbers that are structurally designed to underpin it, magnify its meaning, and amplify its message.

The millions of sinners who have come to Christ based on the clarion and clear revelation of the Word are testimony to the fact that nothing is missing in God's conventional original revelation. Even when translated into all the languages of the world, the Gospel summons men and women to put their faith and trust in Christ — no argument about that.

You can observe a sky scraper and climb its stairs without any knowledge of the steel beams that hold it up, but that does not change the fact that without the steel beams you would not be climbing the stairs.

The reality of the pictures and numbers is that both are embedded in and anchored the meaning of the conventional Hebrew language. This is an undeniable fact. You can ignore it or you can investigate it.

You have been given permission by the Savior Himself to search the Scriptures where you will find the Messiah on every page.

May your search both magnify and increase your love for the Savior who bled and died so that you might have eternal life based on Him and Him alone.

This book is not in competition with the hundreds of ways that God uses to bless, comfort, and encourage His people. It is not for everyone.

But, in our experience, those who have taken the interest and time to investigate the root meaning of the original Hebrew words, both pictures and numbers, report that the experience has been both faith-building and encouraging.

My goal is to encourage the Saints of God. I pray this is a blessing to you!

CHAPTER 12

Hebrew Word Study of Adam

Let's begin our Hebrew picture and number word study by looking at the name of the first man Adam.

Let's investigate:

ADAM   English Translation

ADM   Literal Hebrew

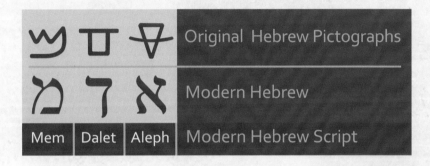

ש	ד	∀	Original Hebrew Pictographs
מ	ד	א	Modern Hebrew
Mem	Dalet	Aleph	Modern Hebrew Script

First Mention

GENESIS 2:19

And out of the ground the Lord God formed every beast of the field, and every fowl of the air; and brought them unto Adam to see what he would call them: and whatsoever Adam called every living creature, that was the name thereof.

Introduction: The day the earth changed! It happened so quickly he could hardly catch his breath. In an instant, it was over!

The succulent juice from the fruit dripped off his chin and landed on the ground with a chilling clap.

The light, that had just moments before brightened his soul, dimmed and finally vanished.

No longer clothed with luminous light, Adam glanced down in shock. His very first thoughts of unworthiness were so gripping that he fell to his knees and covered his eyes.

What was this overwhelming, crushing conviction he suddenly felt?

Shame had entered the garden!

He cringed holding himself tightly, bowed with the stabbing spasm in his chest and stomach.

Pain had entered the garden.

He slowly opened his eyes with his jaw clinched hoping the nightmare would pass. It did not. The heart of Adam was, in one terrible instant, broken. This breach left a chasm so deep it severed the bonds of love and fellowship between himself and his Creator, Elohim.

Sin had invaded the Garden of Eden.

It was a day Adam would never forget nor should we. It was a terrible day that seems to be lost in time.

None of our calendars memorialize this event. Yet, it is the most horrific tragic day in the history of mankind. It is a day that is conspicuous in its absence from the history books or almanacs. Books that chronicle every sort of misery but fail to ever mention the one event that is responsible for all war, disease, sickness, and death. Even the groaning of the earth, which results in earthquakes, fires, tornadoes, tsunamis, floods, pestilence, and a many other miseries, goes unmentioned.

It is the day when paradise was banished from everything except the corrupted imagination and corrupted memories of mankind.

It is the first of many horrific days that were now destined to follow one after another in a parade of sorrows that would go on until it reached the end.

This tragic day should be the headline banner that introduces the ever-growing chronicles of catastrophes.

Sadly, it is not! It is the lost day — a day that goes unnoticed and unheeded.

Adam's SIN-DAY

This day is celebrated the world over in every moment of every day in every man and woman's life since the fall of Adam.

The warning to avoid one forbidden tree, standing alone and solitary, is now multiplied as we see before us forests full of tempting trees laden with the low-hanging forbidden fruit of sin and iniquity.

You are about to embark on an amazing word study that will bring you in contact with the picture and number revelations found in 10 of the most important and amazing words in the Hebrew Scriptures.

It all started with Adam.

Translation of each Picture/Letter in Hebrew Word Adam

ALEPH — Original Hebrew Pictograph of an OX

Aleph is the **1st** letter in the Hebrew Aleph-Beyt. It is pictured as an Ox and means – Strong Leader – First – God the Father.

In the Context of Scripture the symbol Aleph introduces us to Adam, the first of his kind in Creation. He is the Strong Leader who represents all mankind.

DALET — 4 — Door & Creation

Creation – The World – God's Creative works – The Fourth Thing – First number that can be divided – The World – Four Elements – Four Regions of Earth – Four Seasons – Four – Division of Day – Four in Contrast to Seven – Earth (4) vs. Heaven (7) – The Fourth Thing – First Number that can be Divided – Material World that had a Beginning

The second symbol in Adam's name is Dalet. This is a dual revelation that notifies us that Adam is a *creature,* and a *created being* who is going to *open a door* and *enter a pathway.* So far, we know that Adam, the first man, is going to open a door that leads to a pathway for him and all his descendants, including you and me.

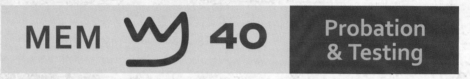

Trials – Probation – Chastisement but not Judgment – Action of Grace Resulting in Revival – Magnified Renewal – An extended Period of Rule or Dominion – Grace multiplied by Eternity (5 x 8) – Working out a Gracious Purpose that has Everlasting Consequences – Probationary Period that results in Renewal.

The final symbol in the name of Adam is clear and the outcome is no longer hidden. We know that Adam ⩒ opened the Door ⊓ that put all mankind on the pathway to chaos, confusion, and death ⱳ.

If that was not enough...

Do you see an amazing prophecy hidden in the very name of Adam?

The first man that opened the door that led to the **MEM** - waters.

Is there a hidden prophecy regarding Noah's flood in the name of Adam?

You decide.

⩒ Adam the first man ⊓ who opened the door that led ⱳ to the *flood.*

CHAPTER 13

Hebrew Word Study of Eden

EDEN   English Translation

EDN   Literal Hebrew

	Original Hebrew Pictographs
	Modern Hebrew
Noon | Dalet | Ayin	Modern Hebrew Script

First Mention

GENESIS 2:8

And the Lord God planted a garden eastward in Eden;

and there he put the man whom he had formed.

Introduction: Have you wondered what Eden was all about? Let's take a look at the Hebrew word Eden and see if it yields up any interesting clues as to the tenure of Adam in the Garden God planted.

Translation of each Picture/Letter in the Hebrew Word Eden

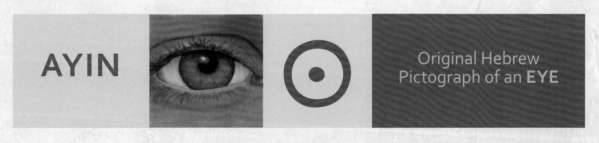

AYIN   Original Hebrew Pictograph of an **EYE**

Ayin is the **16th** letter in the Hebrew Aleph-Beyt. It is pictured as an Eye, and it means – to Understand – Viewing or Seeing – To Know – To Experience.

DALET

Original Hebrew Pictograph of a Pathway or **DOOR**

Dalet is the **4th** letter in the Hebrew Aleph-Beyt. It is pictured as a Pathway or Door and it means – Pathway – Doorway – Gate – Place of Decision – Enterance to Life or Death – Moving into Something – Moving out of Something – To Open – A Place of Change.

NOON

Original Hebrew Pictograph of a Sprout or **FISH**

Noon is the **14th** letter in the Hebrew Aleph-Beyt. It is pictured as a Sprout or a Fish and means – Activity – Life – Constant Motion.

Translation of each Number in Hebrew Word Eden

MEM ⊙ **70** | Experience – Understanding

Punishment and Restoration of Israel – Universality – 7x10 – Perfect Spiritual Order carried out with all Spiritual Power and Significance – the Seventy Nations

NOON **50** | Rest – Deliverance JUBILEE

Holy Spirit - Pentecost – Jubilee – Deliverance followed by Rest

DALET ד 4　Creation

Creation – The World – God's Creative Works – The Fourth Thing – First Number that can be Divided – Four Elements – Four Regions of the Earth – Four Seasons – Four Division of Day – Four in Contrast to Seven – Earth (4) vs. Heaven (7)

Picture & Number Translation of Eden

The man, Created **4** *by God, had the opportunity to Experience* ⊙ *Entering the Path* ד *that leads to* ∼ *Eternal Life. This picture meaning is amplified by* **50***, the number signifying that Deliverance and Jubilee will result in the end. The number* **50** *is the number of multiplied Grace and the gracious work of the Holy Spirit. It is the number connected to Deliverance and Jubilee!*

The one thing the Creator forbade has now become the delight of the created.

In one second, a mouth dripping with the poisonous venom of the forbidden fruit has chased away the light and exchanged it for the darkest of all nights.

The truth cannot be denied or hidden as Adam stands naked and ashamed midst the garden of probation.

Adam has made his choice. And, he made his choice not just for himself. Adam made the choice for all his descendants. He made the choice for all of us.

The doorway and the path that leads to life eternal has been shunned in favor of the door that leads to chaos, confusion, and death.

Eden's doorway is no longer on the earth.

For one brief moment, we hear a hissing sound that echoes throughout the garden. It is the hideous chortling of the self-satisfied serpent.

We are not surprised that Adam and his helpmate, Eve, are driven out of the Garden of Eden. We view with sadness as our first parents venture into a harsh world filled with as many unpleasant surprises as there were secret delights in the Garden of Eden.

But, before we leave the Garden, there is one last encounter with the Creator within the boundaries of the garden of probation.

One small hopeful Sign!

There is also one hopeful sign that is the precursor to the last garden conversation between man and his Creator.

Our adversary, Satan, was created perfect and without defect until iniquity entered his heart. Filled with pride, he imagined himself equal to God. This vainly imagined equality was laden with malice.

To add insult to the folly, Satan foolishly imagined that God was capable of the same petty jealousies and insecurities that had taken root in his own withered heart.

Obsessed by the fever that now piloted his mind, Satan began to maliciously slander the Creator, a pattern of behavior that has continued to this very day.

Satan's slanderous and malicious misrepresentation of God was contagious. It soon took root in the minds of other created angelic beings.

Before long, a third of Heaven's hosts were infected with the rebellious, greedy, self-elevating, and vain spirit that first darkened Satan's mind and heart. It should come as no surprise that this rebellion resulted in Satan being removed from his glorified position of preferment and cast out of Heaven's dominion except as noted in Scripture.

Satan the slanderer is constantly acting as a prosecuting attorney in the courts of Heaven, where he is allowed to bring his accusations against the saints of God. This privilege of access will end abruptly in the middle of the Great Tribulation when God's bailiff, Michael the Archangel, and his security squad throw Satan and his band of rebels out of the courts of Heaven and down to the earth.

This event is closer than you think.

Now, let's get back to our vantage point where we are witnessing the events that are taking place in the Garden of Eden at the moment sin entered the world of man.

Shame, the bitter bread of the Sinner

Contains the kernel of Hope!

I want you to see something!

Take a look at Satan's response to the iniquity that entered his heart and compare it with the response of Adam.

Was Satan filled with remorse?

No, he was filled with an elevated pride and hubris.

Satan felt no shame for his lies and exhibited not even a hint of regret or a sliver of self-doubt.

Satan surely expected Adam to find within his heart that same root of bitterness, hatred, and resentment.

Look how Adam was being cast out of his home in the Garden of Eden.

Adam would surely join Satan as a new recruit in the army pledged to defile all the works of the Creator.

Surely, Adam would be filled with the hot temper of resentment and disdain and, if given the tools, would immediately begin to defile the garden, uproot its bountiful fruit trees and vegetation, molest its animal inhabitants, and fill the place with shrieks and prideful outbursts against the Most-High.

Surely, there would be graffiti in Eden's garden by nightfall, or so thought Satan.

The temptation to sin against the direct command of the Creator had been accomplished masterfully by the serpent.

What happened next must have been a big surprise to Satan.

Adam was not filled with anger and resentment against God.

Adam did not lash out against flora or fauna.

The animals remained unmolested and the garden continued as it had been first created.

This is the first hopeful sign since the disobedient act of rebellion.

Adam was not mad at God but instead was overcome by a crippling sense of sorrow and a desire to find a covering to hide the shocking condition in which he now found himself.

Adam was overcome with **SHAME!**

Instead of comradery with the fallen creature, Satan found himself temporarily abandoned by them as they nursed the overpowering sense of loss and shame.

God graciously pronounced an edict that stands to this day.

There is to be enmity between the serpent and the woman.

Bad Snake, Bad Snake!

The woman Eve, who had heeded the slithering words of the satanically inspired serpent, would have years to ponder all the reasons she should hate and despise the creature that caused her to be deceived and fall into misery.

Satan's desire that the first parents hate and despise God was turned on its head, as our first parents now despised the serpent.

If only Adam's seed had rightly regarded the reason for the calamitous condition of mankind and kept kindled both the sorrow for sin and hatred for the one who caused it — what a different world it would be.

Good Snake, Good Snake!

Sadly, the lies told to Eve have been repackaged and retold so many times by the Father of Lies that mankind almost immediately came back under the seditious spell of Satan. This time they were ready to rebel properly, according to the Luciferian handbook that spews out hatred and bitter accusations against the Most-High.

Consider two simple facts: one anchored in ancient history and the other a daily occurrence.

Consider that the firstborn of Eve was a murderer, and also consider that almost every time a person dies from some unexpected tragedy, God's goodness is questioned.

God is blamed, and His integrity is challenged. He is deemed to be either powerless or secretly malicious.

Good Snake, Bad God?

Every time God is blamed for the results of sin initiated by the evil schemes of Satan, the lie of Satan is advanced.
And what is that lie?

At its very core, it is the following:

God is not really that good.

His words should be heeded with skepticism.

God is keeping mankind from advancing to his full potential.

The Great Irony!

Everything Satan offered Eve, she already had waiting for her as the certain consequence of simple obedience motivated by love for her Creator. Consider the irony!

Eve was under the constant care of a loving God, who had graciously provided for her every need. God's words were trustworthy and meant for the welfare of His creatures.

Eve was already on a path that, left uninterrupted by sin, would have resulted in eternal life in a glorified body.

CHAPTER 14

Hebrew Word Study of Atonement

ATONEMENT   English Translation

KIPPUR   Literal Hebrew

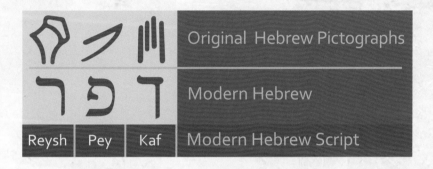

	Original Hebrew Pictographs
פ ר	Modern Hebrew
Reysh	Pey	Kaf	Modern Hebrew Script

Introduction: The Day of Atonement or Yom Kippur was a ceremony initiated by God Himself. It began immediately after the deaths of Nadab and Abihu. These two sons of Aaron attempted to improve upon God's instructions for temple offerings. They had decided to add their own un-authorized fire offering to the Lord.

The Lord was not pleased with the "strange fire" the two sons of Aaron presumptuously offered in His presence. Their lives were taken and a great lesson regarding the *holiness* of God was temporarily learned.

Immediately after this event, God came to Moses and gave specific instructions regarding what the Lord called a **DAY of ATONEMENT.**

You can read the details of this in the 16th chapter of the book of Leviticus.

Even to this day, among the Jews The Day of Atonement is considered the most holy day in the entire year. The day is preceded by 10 days of fasting and prayer. The final day of these days of affliction ends on Tishri 10, the Day of Atonement.

While the Day of Atonement is still observed by the Jews, it is impossible for them to observe it as commanded by the Lord for the following reasons:

The Aaronic priesthood no longer functions. Because it does not presently exist it cannot perform the detailed rituals set out by God. Even if they did exist, the priesthood would be unable to memorialize the 10th of Tishri as prescribed by God because there is no longer a tabernacle or a temple.

The holy sanctuary was destroyed by the Romans in 70 AD.

The congregation no longer congregates, the altar on which the sacrifices were to take place no longer exists, and the sacrifices ceased in the latter half of the first century AD.

The scarlet cord is no longer tied around the temple door on the Day Atonement. The scarlet cord that miraculously turned white as a sign from Heaven that atonement had been made.

The temple door no longer exists.

The scapegoat is no longer sent out of Jerusalem to die in the wilderness.

The Day of Atonement as prescribed by God no longer exists.

Despite the fact that the Day of Atonement can no longer be celebrated in the way prescribed by God, the day still remains as the most holy day of the year for religious Jews. It has been kept alive by observant Jews as best they are able considering that all the ceremonies, priests, offerings, altars, and geography that were necessary to carry out the strict instructions of the Lord God of Israel are either destroyed or in disarray.

There is one thing however that remains unchanged.

The one absolutely necessary thing that is able, once understood, to guide you to the place where full atonement can be found once and for all time.

This is the atonement that is absolutely necessary for anyone who wishes to spend eternity in the presence of the holy God of Israel.

This one thing can be discovered in one word.

It is a word that has a message hidden in it that can provide for the person who understands and by faith receives the atonement gift that has been graciously provided by the God of Israel.

Wouldn't you like to know how to have your sins blotted out and remembered no more?

The one word is *Kippur.* The word that is literally translated in Hebrew as propitation and is translated into English as *atonement.*

Now let's take a look at the miraculous message hidden in plain sight just under the three letters that compose one of the most amazing words in all of Scripture. The word **Kippur**.

The word translated in the English Bible as *atonement.*

The three letters in the Hebrew word Kippur are Kaf, Pey and Reysh.

Now let's see what is hidden in the three pictures that undergird these three Hebrew letters.

The first letter in Kippur is Kaf. It is pictured as an open hand. The meaning of the picture is the palm of the hand that covers, or provides a covering, or that opens and allows something to be released.

It is the one letter that is connected with the concept of atonement or propitiation.

We are going to reveal this truth in the same way it was originally written as the language first dictated to Moses by YHVH picture/letter by picture/letter. This pure language spoken of by Zephaniah is the language we know today as Hebrew — the orriginal language of the Garden of Eden.

Translation of each Picture/Letter in the Hebrew Word Atonement

The First Picture/Letter in the Hebrew word **Kippur** is the letter **Kaf.**

Kaf is the **11th** letter in the Hebrew Aleph-Beyt. It is pictured as an open Hand, Palm out and means – To Cover – A Cover – To Open – To Allow.

The Second Picture/Letter in the Hebrew word **Kippur** is the letter **Pey.**

Pey is the **17th** letter in the Hebrew Aleph-Beyt. It is pictured as an open Mouth and means – To Speak – A Word – To Open – Mouth – To Cover.

REYSH — Original Hebrew Pictograph of PRINCE

The Third pictured/Letter in the Hebrew word **Kippur** is letter **Reysh.**

Reysh is pictured as the Head Person.

Reysh is the **20th** letter in the Hebrew Aleph-Beyt. It is pictured as a Head Person or Prince and means – A Person – The Head – The Highest – Leader – The Sum – The Supreme – The First – The Most Important – The Top – Master – Prince.

Picture Translation of the Atonement

The *Prince* or *Judge* that is about to declare judgment on a criminal but instead *Covers* his *Mouth* and refuses to pass sentence on the convicted criminal.

| Reysh | Pey | Kaf | Original Hebrew Pictographs — Modern Hebrew |

Translation of each Number in Hebrew Word Atonement
(Based on Biblical Usage)

KAF ‖‖ **20** REDEMPTION

10 x 2 – Magnified Ordinal Perfection & Redemption

PEY ✓ 80 ETERNITY

10 x 8 - Magnified Ordinal Perfection & Eternity
New Beginnings and New Birth

REYSH ⬗ 200 SUFFICIENCY of God & Insufficiency

10 x 20 - Magnified Ordinal Perfection & Redemption
Redemption of Body and Soul – Multiplied by Ordinal Perfection –
Accomplished by the Son of God – Sufficient to Accomplish a Purpose –
Ransom that is both Efficient and Sufficient to Reclaim what was
Lost – To Accomplish Redemption

Number Translation of the Atonement

⬗	✓	⦀	Original Hebrew Pictographs
Reysh	Pey	Kaf	Modern Hebrew Script
200	80	20	Modern Hebrew Numbers

Redemption and eternal life are out of man's reach. Man is completely incapable of saving himself and apart from Divine intervention is doomed and damned.

So, let's take a minute and look at what we have learned so far about the Hebrew word Kippur based on the pictures and numbers.

We learn from the number meaning that the criminal is not standing before an earthly judge. He is on trial for the destiny of his very soul. He is standing before the One who can send him to Heaven or Hell. The crimes he has committed are crimes that send the offenders to Hell. He can offer no defense for himself as he hangs his head awaiting his death sentence. But, then suddenly, there is silence in the courtroom as the Judge puts his hand over his mouth and refuses to pass sentence of the guilty criminal.

In order to discover what happens next, we need to take a look at the one number that is displayed by Kippur.

There is one Final Number in the Hebrew Word Atonement

If you asked a Jew to tell you what number he sees when he looks at the word Kippur (Kaf, Pey, Reysh), you would expect he would tell you that he sees the number 20, the number 80, and the number 200.

But that is not what he sees. He sees...

SHEEN **W** 300

Kaf 20 + Pey 80 + Reysh 200 = **SHEEN 300**

So, what does **300,** the sum number of the Hebrew word Kippur mean?

Three Hundred (300 W) turns out to be one of the most amazing numbers in all of Scripture.

The meaning of Hebrew numbers can only be understood by searching the Scriptures alone in order to find out how and in what context the number is used.

In order to discover the meaning of the number 300 we need to investigate every time the number 300 is used in the Bible.

GENESIS 5:22

Enoch and the Number (W 300) – Number of years Enoch walked with God before he was not, because God took him to Heaven. – **GENESIS 5:22**

Noah and the Number (W 300) – The length in cubits of Noah's ark.
GENESIS 6:15

Gideon and the Number (W 300) – And the Lord said unto Gideon, By the three hundred men that lapped will I save you, and deliver the Midianites into thine hand. **JUDGES 6-7**

Sampson and the Number (W 300) – **JUDGES 15:4**

King David and the Number (W 300) – **1 CHRONICLES 11:11**

Enoch, Noah, Gideon, Samson, and David with his mighty men all had great victories. The thing that makes these three conquests unusual is that they can only be understood as you see the hand of God giving a **supernatural victory over enemies and death itself.**

Does the number 300 show up in the New Testament?

The answer is yes!

*Jesus Christ and the Number () – Mary of Bethany
who anointed the body of Jesus just before His crucifixion
is connected to the Number 300.*

MARK 14:5

*For it might have been sold for more than three
hundred pence, and have been given to the poor.
And they murmured against her.*

The meaning of the number 300 in this story is immediately understood by simply reading the response of Jesus.

MARK 14:6-9

*And Jesus said, Let her alone; why trouble ye her? She hath wrought
a good work on me. For ye have the poor with you always, and
whomsoever ye will ye may do them good: but me ye have not
always. She hath done what she could: she is come a forehand to
anoint my body to the burying. Verily I say unto you, Wheresoever
this gospel shall be preached throughout the whole world, this also
that she hath done shall be spoken of for a memorial of her.*

If we were to describe the meaning of the number 300, based on this verse alone, we might translate the meaning as follows:

*The number 300 is a proclamation of the death and burial
of Yeshua Ha-Mashiach, the Lord Jesus the Christ.*

Jesus discloses that this story, including the number 300, is going to be published as a part of the gospel narrative as it is preached throughout the world.

So, to be clear, the number is not only associated with death and burial but also the good news that Christ is risen!

The number 300 is an awesome numeric reminder of the price that was paid for our redemption.

A summarization of all the verses could read as follows:

We have a certain hope that we will have victory over the final enemy of death, all because of the death, burial, and resurrection of Yeshua Ha-Mashiach, Jesus the Christ.

Now let's add what we have learned from the sum number of Kippur, the number 300.

Summary of Picture and Numbers of Atonement

We learn from the number meaning that the criminal is not standing before an earthly judge. He is on trial for the destiny of his very soul. He is standing before the Lord of Heaven, who can send him to Heaven or Hell.

The sinner can offer no defense for himself, as he hangs his head awaiting his death sentence. But, then suddenly, there is silence in the courtroom as the Lord puts His hand over His mouth and refused to pass sentence of the guilty criminal.

Someone has to pay the penalty for the sin of the criminal.

The Lord, who has never committed any crime, who is perfect and without sin, finally takes His hand away from His mouth and announces that He is the only one who can atone for the sins of the guilty sinner.

He announces that He will take the sinner's place, and He will take upon Himself all the sinner's iniquity.

The sinner is declared *not guilty!* The sinner, by God's grace, has been granted a supernatural victory over the last enemy, death. This was made possible by the meritorious work that Jesus Christ, the spotless Lamb of God, accomplished on the Cross of Calvary and by his efficient resurrection from death. His resurrected life is the surety of the resurrection and everlasting life He promised to all those who put their trust in Him, and Him alone.

CHAPTER 15

Hebrew Word Study of God

GOD

English Translation

ELOHIM

Literal Hebrew

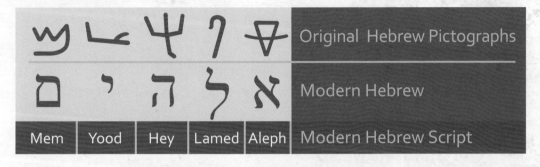

					Original Hebrew Pictographs
					Modern Hebrew
Mem	Yood	Hey	Lamed	Aleph	Modern Hebrew Script

First Mention

GENESIS 1:1

In the beginning GOD Created the heaven and the earth.

Introduction: Let me introduce you to your Creator who has revealed Himself by name over 34 times in the first chapter of Genesis. It is only after introducing Himself as Elohim 35 times that He reveals that His name is also YHVH.

Elohim has also graciously disclosed the meaning of His name in pictures and numbers in order that you might understand and be wise.

It is no accident that Elohim is the third word in the first verse of the literal revelation we find in the ancient prophetic Scriptures known as the book of Genesis.

Elohim is the name we translate into English as *God.* The name Elohim is revealed 35 times between **Genesis 1:1** and **Genesis 2:4**.

YHVH, the second name God purposely revealed to man, is first declared in **Genesis 2:4**.

*These are the generations of the heavens and of the earth when they were created, in the day that **YHVH** (the Lord) **ELOHIM** (God) made the earth and the heavens.*

Whenever you see the title God in your English Bible you should remember that behind that title is the name Elohim.

Whenever you see the title capitalized or emboldened word LORD in your English Bible you should remember that behind that title is the name YHVH.

The name Elohim is the first name revealed in the Scripture.

The name is revealed over 4000 times in Scriptures.

Please, be mindful that His name as Creator is Elohim.

The connection between Creator and Elohim is not always obvious in the conventional Hebrew translation of the name Elohim. The meaning becomes undeniable once you read the picture and number language hidden in the plain Hebrew text.

Sadly, the meaning of Elohim is completely lost in the English translation.

Translation of each Picture/Letter in Hebrew Word ELOHIM

ALEPH   Original Hebrew Pictograph of an OX

Aleph is the **1st** letter in the Hebrew Aleph-Beyt. It is pictured as an Ox and means – Strong Leader – First – God the Father.

LAMED

Original Hebrew
Pictograph of a STAFF

Lamed is the **12th** letter in the Hebrew Aleph-Beyt.
It is pictured as a Staff and means – Essence of Authority
and Control – A Tongue that speaks Words –
The Shepherd's Staff – The Voice of Authority –
To Speak with Authority – The Son.

Who was the voice of authority that spoke the worlds into existence
with His words?

JOHN 1: 1-3

*In the beginning was the Word, and the Word was with God,
and the Word was God. The same was in the beginning with God.
All things were made by him; and without him was not
anything made that was made*

HEY

Original Hebrew
Pictograph to BEHOLD

Hey is the **5th** letter in the Hebrew Aleph-Beyt.
It is pictured as a man with arms raised and means – Reveal –
The Revealer – Look – Behold – The Holy Spirit.

Who, together with the Father and the Son, accomplished the amazing
work of creation?

YOOD — Original Hebrew Pictograph of a HAND

Yood is the **10th** letter in the Hebrew Aleph-Beyt. It is pictured as a hand and means – To Work – A Mighty Deed – To Make – Divine Deed.

MEM — Original Hebrew Pictograph of WATERS

Mem is the **13th** letter in the Hebrew Aleph-Beyt. It is pictured as water and means: Liquid – Massive – Chaos – Living Water – Waters.

Picture Translation of Elohim
Our Creator

God the Father

God the Son

God the Holy Spirit

Accomplished a Divine Deed

Separating the Waters from the Waters

𐤀 God the Father, 𐤉 God the Son, and Ψ God the Holy Spirit accomplished a 𐤋 Divine Deed by separating the ꟼ Waters from the Waters.

Elohim's purpose was to make a home for man and the rest of His creation on the dry ground, the waters, and the heaven above the earth. It was all good.

Number Translation of Elohim

ELOHIM
Literal Hebrew

ꟼ	𐤋	Ψ	𐤉	𐤀	Original Hebrew Pictographs
Mem	Yood	Hey	Lamed	Aleph	Modern Hebrew Script
40	100	5	30	1	Modern Hebrew Numbers

ALEPH 𐤀 1   God the Father

Deity – Unity – Complete Self Sufficiency – Independence – The First – Indivisible – The First Cause of Everything else

LAMED � 30	Blood Sacrifice

Blood of Christ – Dedication – 3x10 Magnified Divine Perfection of A Divine Plan unveiled at just the Right Moment

HEY ψ 5	Grace

God's Goodness – The Revelation in the First Five Books of the Bible – Divine Strength – Unmerited Favor

YOOD ∟ 10	Ordinal Perfection

Perfection of Divine Order – Completeness of Order – Testimony – The Law – Responsibility – A Plan Ordained in Heaven that is accomplished on earth at the Appointed Time

MEM ש 40	Probation & Testing

Trials – Chastisement but not Judgment – Action of Grace resulting in Revival – Magnified Renewal – An extended Period of Rule or Dominion – Grace multiplied by Eternity (5 x 8) – Working out a Gracious Purpose that has Everlasting Consequences

Now let's look at the meaning of the numbers that make up the Hebrew word, Elohim.

∀ 1 God provides a � 30 Blood Sacrifice that is ψ 5 revealed by His Grace at ∟ 10 exactly the Divinely Appointed Time in order to provide revival, renewal, and salvation to man who has ש 40 failed his Probationary Test, and is now humbly looking to the Messiah the Son of God for salvation and redemption.

Where the First Adam Failed
the Last Adam Succeeds!

There is much to learn from the revelation of the name of God, Elohim. It unmasks the first amazing truth regarding the gracious intentions of our Creator and is foundational to our understanding our relationship to God.

It also introduces us to **Lamed**  the second picture corresponding with the second person in the Trinity. He is *The One Who Speaks with Authority* and is pictured holding the Shepherd Staff.

Who is He?

He is our Creator, and He is the Messiah. He is the Son of God, who laid down His life for His sheep in order that we might be welcomed as sons and daughters into Heaven based on His sacrificial atonement made on our behalf.

And, what should be our response?

Believe and Receive!

CHAPTER 16

Hebrew Word Study of Moses

MOSES

English Translation

MOSHE

Literal Hebrew

	Original Hebrew Pictographs
	Modern Hebrew
Hey | Sheen | Mem	Modern Hebrew Script

First Mention

EXODUS 2:10

*And the child grew, and she brought him unto Pharaoh's daughter,
and he became her son. And she called his name **MOSES**:
and she said, Because I drew him out of the water.*

Introduction: Moses is the one man mentioned more often than any other man in the Scriptures.

There is little doubt that the Children of Israel, who were miraculously led out of the bondage of Egypt by Almighty God, were familiar with the meaning of the name of Moses. Moses was drawn out of the Nile river by the daughter of pharaoh and adopted into the royal family at the same time that Israelites were slaves in Egypt.

The name Moses bears witness to that miracle of deliverance from the water.

Moses was appointed and given authority by God to accomplish his mission as revealed by God.

Moses was a type of the coming Messiah, the Appointed One. Moses was appointed by God to deliver His people from the bondage of Egypt.

To discover the meaning of the name Moses, we need to investigate the pictures and numbers of the three Hebrew letters that compose the name.

Keep in mind that what is now called Hebrew is the language given to Adam as a gift in Garden of Eden and was designed from the beginning to reveal, amplify, and magnify the Son of God.

Translation of each Picture/Letter in Hebrew Word Moses

HEY   SHEEN   MEM

MEM  Original Hebrew Pictograph of **WATER**

Mem is the **13th** letter of the Hebrew Aleph-Beyt. It is pictured as Water and means – Liquid – Mighty Waters like the Ocean – Massive as the Waves of the Sea – Chaotic and Destructive like a Tsunami – Life-giving as Rain or the Clear Water found in a Well or a Brook.

The first letter in the name of Moses is Mem. Mem is pictured as Water. It can picture the calm water of a life-giving stream or the gentle rain that showers the earth, so that it might bring forth its bounty. Or, it can picture the violent and chaotic water of the ocean that brings destruction and death by way of floods and tsunamis. Water can be a picture of life or it can be a picture of death and destruction, chaos, and confusion.

SHEEN   **W**   Original Hebrew Pictograph of **TEETH**

Sheen is the **21st** letter in the Hebrew Aleph-Beyt. It is pictured as Teeth and means – To Consume – To Destroy – Sharp – To Press The One Letter that God used to identify Himself God's Signature – the Letter that stands for God Almighty.

The second letter in the name of Moses is Sheen. Sheen is pictured as Teeth. Sheen is a picture of pressing or gnashing. It can be the picture of destruction or of unmatched formidable power and strength. It is the one letter that God uses as His signature. It is an awesome and mysterious letter that should cause the reader to take special note of its meaning.

HEY

Original Hebrew Pictograph of **TO BEHOLD**

Hey is the **5th** letter in the Hebrew Aleph-Beyt. It is pictured as a Man with Arms Raised to the Heavens and means – Pay Attention to what Follows – To Reveal – To Unfold – To Look Upon Holy Spirit as the Revelator – To Behold.

The third, and final, letter in the name of Moses is the letter Hey. The letter Hey is pictured as a man lifting up his hands to Heaven. It is the picture of either proclaiming or receiving a revelation. It is a number often associated with God the Holy Spirit, the Great Revelator.

Picture Translation of the name Moses

The picture meaning of the name of Moses is not very difficult to decipher.

The revelation **Hey** Ψ is that chaos, confusion, destruction, and death **Mem** ᗰ will be themselves destroyed **Sheen** W. Or, put another way, the suffering and slavery, the bondage and death **Mem** ᗰ being experienced by the Children of Israel in Egypt was going to be victoriously vanquished **Sheen** W. This was the *message* or *revelation of hope* to Israel **Hey** Ψ embedded in the name of Moses.

147

God is the one who sovereignly ordained the destiny of Moses in order to rescue His people from the bondage of Egypt. A bondage that had accomplished its purpose and was now a stumbling block to the greater purpose of God.

The greater purpose for Israel was brought about by the sovereign hand of God who raised up and anointed Moses. His very name and the numbers in his name disclosed God's purpose.

Moses was also a picture of the coming Messiah, who would deliver all those that trusted Him from the bondage of sin and death.

This promise is being fulfilled in the Gentile nations of the world, and it's awaits it final fulfillment in these last days, when God will take the blinders off of Israel and they will clearly see that Yeshua Ha-Mashiach is their Messiah.

This final revelation, of the Messiah, will come at the end of a time of sorrow and trouble, that makes the bondage in Egypt pale by comparison.

But, the promise is that in the end all remaining Israel, who will one day soon finally recognize their Salvation is Yeshua, will *all* be saved. What a day that will be — a day not far off.

Translation of each Number in Hebrew Word MOSES

MOSES
English Translation

Ψ	W	ꖉ	Original Hebrew Pictographs
Hey	Sheen	Mem	Modern Hebrew Script
5	300	40	Modern Hebrew Numbers

*Trials – Chastisement but not Judgment – Action of
Grace resulting in Revival – Magnified Renewal –
an extended Period of Rule or Dominion –
Grace multiplied by Eternity (5 x 8) –
Working out a Gracious Purpose that
has Everlasting Consequences*

The first number in the name of Moses is ꟽ **40.** Forty is the number that means probation. It is a number that signifies a period of testing that is going to be followed by deliverance and salvation.

We all know that the Children of Israel wandered for forty years in the wilderness as a result of their unbelief.

At the end of the 40 years of probation and testing, Israel returned to the Promised Land under the leadership of Joshua and Caleb, who as spies 40 years earlier brought back a good report of the Promised Land. In this, we see them as two more types of the coming Messiah.

SHEEN W 300   Supernatural Victory over the Enemy

*Supernatural Victory Over Enemies Including Death.
A Divinely Appointed Period of Time – Election – Number Connected
to the "Children of Promise" – The Death, Burial and Resurrection
of Messiah – Signifies final Blood Sacrifice accomplished
by the Spotless Lamb of God*

The second letter, which is also a number in the name of Moses, is Sheen W or the number **300.** The number **300** is one of the most amazing numbers in the Scriptures.

It is the number first associated with the "catching away" of Enoch.

It is the number of one of the dimensions of Noah's ark — the wooden instrument that God designed in order that mankind be preserved and delivered from the flood.

It is the number of Gideon's army — the army that won a miraculous victory over the enemy.

It is a number associated with Sampson and his victory over the Philistines.

It is the number associated with King David and his victories over the enemies of Israel.

The Scriptures also clearly use the number **300** as the picture of destruction. Three hundred is the number that reveals the awesome power of God over His enemies. It is also the number that reminds us of the grace of God as the defender of His children.

The final picture of the number **300** is found in the New Testament.

It is a number that Yeshua the Messiah said would always be associated with the good news of the Gospel.

The number 300 will be forever connected to the anointing of Yeshua Ha-Mashiach's body for burial. It is the number that reminds us that Yeshua rose from the dead. Three hundred is the number that amazes us with the miracle of the resurrection of Jesus the Christ and comforts us while we, who trust in the finished work of the Messiah, will also be resurrected from the dead. Sheen W, the number 300, is the one number that signifies victory over death - the Resurrection!

God's Goodness – What Follows Creation – Pentateuch – Divine Strength – Unmerited Favor – *Grace*

The third letter in the Hebrew name Moses is the letter Hey ᴪ, which is also the number 5.

Summary Translation of the Numbers in MOSES

Let's see what is revealed based on the three numbers disclosed in the name of Moses.

Forty reveals that there is going to be a time of testing and probation.

The Scriptures reveal that the Children of Israel wandered for **40** years in the wilderness as a result of their unbelief. We also know that at the end of the **40** years of probation and testing, Israel entered the Promised land under the leadership of the two spies, who forty years earlier brought back a good report. In Joshua and Caleb we see two more examples of the coming Messiah.

The number **300** reveals that God's children will be given miraculous victories over the enemies of both God and Israel.

Five is the one number that is used in Scripture to signify grace and mercy.

The pictures in the name of Moses, have a prophetic meaning that will be disclosed in the future when the Messiah comes to earth to do the will of His Heavenly Father.

As we look at the name of Moses who is a type of Christ, through the Messianic lens of Scripture, based on the numbers that have a meaning exclusively based on how they are used in Scripture.

Forty reveals that there is going to be a time of testing and probation for mankind. A probationary period and a test that every human being, from Adam to the most righteous men to ever live, have *all* failed miserably.

This probationary period of testing has only been successfully overcome by one individual.

The name of that individual is Jesus the Christ, Yeshua Ha-Mashiach, the one appointed by God to pass the one test for man that no man could pass on his own merit.

The deliverance and salvation that follows the number **40** is only possible because of Jesus the Christ lived the perfect life demanded by His righteous Holy Father. This qualified Jesus to be the spotless Lamb of God, who had been appointed to take away the sin of the world.

Three Hundred reveals that a time of final deliverance is coming. Deliverance from the bondage of sin and the wrath of God. And, we know that this time forecast for deliverance has come.

We are now almost 2000 years past the event that God designed to be the center point of all mankind. The time when *sin* and *death* were vanquished on a rough wooden cross on which His own Son died, so that man might live.

Five reveals that this is all of God's grace and that man can do no work on his own to earn the gift that God offered on the cross of Calvary.

Although, man cannot do any work to deserve God's approval, still God does demand that man do *one work* in order to receive this free gift of eternal life.

And what is that *work*?

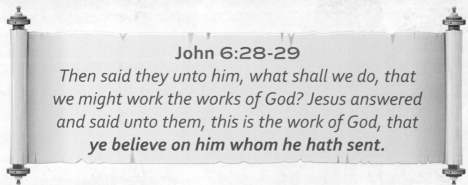

John 6:28-29

Then said they unto him, what shall we do, that we might work the works of God? Jesus answered and said unto them, this is the work of God, that **ye believe on him whom he hath sent.**

Let's summarize the numeric meaning of the Hebrew name we translate into English as Moses.

40 We have all experienced a time of testing and probation and we have all failed the test. But, God in His great mercy promises us both deliverance and salvation.

300 A supernatural victory over death and sin has come at a great price and at great expense to our Heavenly Father. It is a price that none of us could ever pay since God could not be enticed by all the riches of this world to give us His Only Begotten Son as a sin offering. Yet, His great love has produced a gift to mankind that no amount of treasure could ever buy.

Moses is a faint shadow picture of the Messiah. And, the number 300 in his name is a harbinger of the death, burial, and resurrection of the Messiah. This is the foundation of what we call the Good News or Gospel of Jesus the Christ.

5 reminds us that all of this is a result of freely given, undeserved favor.

The numbers in Moses are a harbinger of the coming Messiah, who has delivered us from the pain and penalty of sin and hell by shedding His precious blood as an atonement for our sin. This free gift is offered to all who will simply put their faith and trust in the risen Messiah, Yeshua Ha-Mashiach.

CHAPTER 17

Hebrew Word Study of Jerusalem

JERUSALEM   English Translation

IRUSHLM   Literal Hebrew

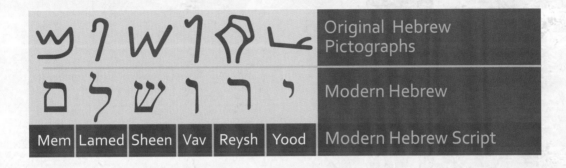

						Original Hebrew Pictographs
מ	ל	ש	ו	ר	י	Modern Hebrew
Mem	Lamed	Sheen	Vav	Reysh	Yood	Modern Hebrew Script

First Mention

JOSHUA 10:1

Now it came to pass, when Adonizedec king of Jerusalem had heard how Joshua had taken Ai, and had utterly destroyed it; as he had done to Jericho and her king, so he had done to Ai and her king; and how the inhabitants of Gibeon had made peace with Israel, and were among them;

Introduction: Modern Jerusalem is the capital city of Israel. It is an ancient holy city and a center of pilgrimage for Jews, Christians, and Muslims. It was divided between Israel and Jordan in 1948. The Jordanian sector was annexed by Israel after the 1967 war.

Jerusalem has been the capital of Israel since 1950. And, it was recognized by the United States and many other countries as the official capital of Israel in December of 2017.

The first time Jerusalem is mentioned is in Joshua 10:1. It is ruled by a pagan king named Adonizedec. He is not just an ordinary pagan king; he is one of 22 giants mentioned in the Scriptures.

By the time you get to the 43rd verse of Joshua Chapter 10, Jerusalem is no longer ruled by the wicked king Adonizedec.

What happens in between is one of the most exciting and miraculous accounts in all of the Scripture. There is no question that Joshua 10:1-43 has prophetic implications that are harbingers of the last days, the final days before the coming of the Messiah to set up His Millennial Kingdom.

Listen to some of the strange and supernatural events that took place as recorded in the book of Joshua. Some of the elements of the account in Joshua 10 include: the sun and moon standing still, the kings of the earth hiding in caves, the destruction of the corrupted pagans by hailstones, and the siege of Jerusalem.

Do these events sound strangely familiar?

If you read the book of Revelation, you will find many parallel accounts that God promises to unfold during the terminal generation who occupies the earth just prior to the second coming of the Messiah.

And, before you start feeling too sorry for all the wicked inhabitants of Jerusalem, who were destroyed by Joshua, keep in mind that these kingdoms that came against Israel were corrupted. They were not just morally corrupt but they actually had their DNA corrupted, and many were themselves hybridized - part human part Nephilim (fallen angels). Many of the Canaanites had become unrecognizable to the Creator, as they were a creature He had not created. The corruption was ubiquitous.

Keep in mind that *pattern* is very often *prophecy*.

Jesus told us that the last days would be like the days of Noah. In other words, mankind would have again corrupted himself or been corrupted by fallen angels and demons.

I would encourage you to read for your self the biblical account and connect the dots to the headlines that are now unfolding in present day Jerusalem.

Can we read the headlines in any paper in any capital of the world and find the fulfillment of end time's prophecy? Are there prophecies unique to the last 70 years of this present age? Do we see prophecies that center around Israel and Jerusalem?

Are we witnessing prophecies that could only be fulfilled after the children of Israel miraculously returned to the land of Israel in 1948 and again occupied Jerusalem in 1967?

Are there prophecies that could not have been fulfilled between 70 AD and 1948, when the land of Israel was invaded and the children of Israel scattered to the four corners of the world? Could there be prophecies that would only unfold once Israel was re-established *one day* as a nation, as foretold in Isaiah 66:8?

Listen to what the prophet Isaiah revealed:

> *Who hath heard such a thing? who hath seen such things? Shall the earth be made to bring forth **in one day?** or shall a **nation** be born at once? for as soon as Zion travailed, she brought forth her children.*

This prophecy was further fulfilled when Israel gained possession of their most precious earthly inheritance - *Jerusalem!*

And, what is in store for Jerusalem now that God has brought His people back to the land?

This prophecy was fulfilled on May 14, 1948. And, you could have read about it in any paper from any capital city in the world. This headlne was published in advance by God, and reported by His prophet Zechariah in 580 BC — nearly 2500 years before it happened!

ZECHARIAH 12:2-3

Behold, I will make Jerusalem a cup of trembling unto all the people round about, when they shall be in the siege both against Judah and against Jerusalem.

And in that day will I make Jerusalem a burdensome stone for all people: all that burden themselves with it shall be cut in pieces, though all the people of the earth be gathered together against it.

Twin Pictorial Translations of the Word Jerusalem

The battle for Jerusalem, one of the oldest and the most contested piece of real estate in the history of the world, did *not* begin with the first Crusade sanctioned by Pope Urban 11 in 1095 AD.

The battle for Jerusalem is ancient and very significant, as you are about to discover.

Genesis 14:18 makes the first mention of a city called Salem. Most Jewish commentators believe this refers to Jerusalem, ruled by King Melchizedek.

The name Melchizedek is mentioned in both the Old Testament and the New Testament and is believed to be a "shadow type" of the Messiah. His name is reported to mean **"My King is Righteous."**

According to the Midrash (Jewish tradition), Jerusalem was founded by Shem and Eber, the forefathers of Abraham.

This would put the founding of Jerusalem immediately after the worldwide flood of Noah, somewhere around 2700 BC.

According to the Bible, the Israelites' history connected with Jerusalem in 1000 BC when King David occupied Jerusalem. Biblical evidence for temporarily destroying the city of Jerusalem is recorded much earlier, as Joshua is reported to have conquered the city and killed its king shortly after entering the Promised Land. But, Joshua did not occupy Jerusalem, and it remained under the control of the Jebusites until the 7th year or the reign of King David, who captured and inhabited the city for the last 33 years of his reign.

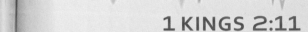

1 KINGS 2:11

And the days that David reigned over Israel were forty years: seven years reigned he in Hebron, and thirty and three years reigned he in Jerusalem.

While there is disagreement about which city is the "oldest city" in the world based on "continuous habitation", there is no question that Jerusalem is the most contested city in all of history.

During its long history, Jerusalem has been destroyed twice, besieged 23 times, attacked 52 times, and captured then recaptured 44 times.

The Bible first mentions Jerusalem in the 10th chapter of Joshua. This account holds the secret for understanding the hidden meaning and prophetic significance of Jerusalem. We will discover in the pictorial and numeric meaning that this is the foundation for the Hebrew word Jerusalem.

You cannot begin to fathom the enormous significance of Jerusalem until you understand one over-arching reality. It is the stunning reality that Abraham first glimpsed. It was a vision that seeded and watered his faith. It was a vision that made God smile on Abraham and bless him above all men. And, what was that vision that bolstered his faith and made God smile with pleasure?

Abraham was a pilgrim in this world, and he had his eyes not on any earthly city but on a city whose maker and builder was God.

HEBREWS 11:8-10

By faith Abraham, when he was called to go out into a place which he should after receive for an inheritance, obeyed; and he went out, not knowing whither he went. By faith he sojourned in the land of promise, as in a strange country, dwelling in tabernacles with Isaac and Jacob, the heirs with him of the same promise: For he looked for a city which hath foundations, whose builder and maker is God.

HEBREWS 11:13-16

These all died in faith, not having received the promises, but having seen them afar off, and were persuaded of them, and embraced them, and confessed that they were strangers and pilgrims on the earth. For they that say such things declare plainly that they seek a country. And truly, if they had been mindful of that country from whence they came out, they might have had opportunity to have returned. But now they desire a better country, that is, an heavenly: wherefore God is not ashamed to be called their God: for he hath prepared for them a city.

And, what was the name of the city that Abraham was envisioning by faith?

What is the name of the city that God has prepared for those that were strangers and pilgrims on the earth?

What was the blessed vision of those that received the promises of God by faith?

The answer is found in the last book of the Scriptures.

REVELATION 3:12

*Him that overcometh will I make a pillar in the temple of my God, and he shall go no more out: and I will write upon him the name of my God, and the name of the city of my God, which is new **Jerusalem,** which cometh down out of heaven from my God:*

REVELATION 21:2

*And I John saw the holy city, new **Jerusalem,** coming down from God out of heaven, prepared as a bride adorned for her husband.*

REVELATION 21:10

*And he carried me away in the spirit to a great and high mountain, and shewed me that great city, the holy **Jerusalem,** descending out of heaven from God.*

And, what is the future for Jerusalem prior to the New Jerusalem descending upon the earth from heaven?

The Scriptures foretell the glorious end of the earthly city called Jerusalem. Jerusalem will be established in peace and righteousness for 1000 years.

And, what will Jerusalem be called in this millennial period where Jerusalem is the capital of the entire world?

The answer is found in **the Old Testament book of Jeremiah**.

JEREMIAH 3:17

*At that time they shall call **Jerusalem** the throne of the Lord; and all the nations shall be gathered unto it, to the name of the Lord, to **Jerusalem:** neither shall they walk any more after the imagination of their evil heart.*

Translation of each Picture/Letter
in the Hebrew Word Jerusalem

JERUSALEM

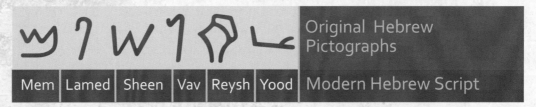

Mem	Lamed	Sheen	Vav	Reysh	Yood	Modern Hebrew Script

Original Hebrew Pictographs

YOOD
Original Hebrew Pictograph of HAND

Yood is the **10th** letter in the Hebrew Aleph-Beyt. It is pictured as a Hand and means - To Work – A Mighty Deed – To Make – Divine Deed.

REYSH
Original Hebrew Pictograph of PRINCE

Reysh is the **20th** letter in the Hebrew Aleph-Beyt. It is pictured as the Head Person and means – A Person – The Head – The Highest – Leader – The Sum – The Supreme – The First – The Most Important – The Top – Master – Prince.

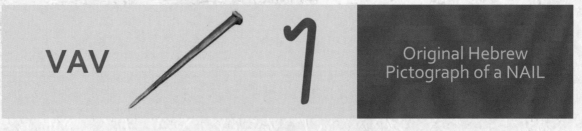

VAV
Original Hebrew Pictograph of a NAIL

Vav is the **6th** letter in the Hebrew Aleph-Beyt.
It is pictured as an Iron Nail or a Wooden Hook or a Peg and means – To Add one Thing to Another – To Secure.

SHEEN

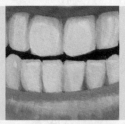

Original Hebrew Pictograph of Supernatural VICTORY over the Enemy

Sheen is the **21st** letter in the Hebrew Aleph-Beyt. It is pictured as Teeth and means – Supernatural Victory Over Enemies *Including Death* – A Divinely Appointed Period of Time – Election – Number Connected to the "Children of Promise" – The Death, Burial, and Resurrection of Messiah – Signifies final Blood Sacrifice accomplished by the Spotless Lamb of God.

LAMED

Original Hebrew Pictograph of a STAFF

Lamed is the **12th** letter in the Hebrew Aleph-Beyt. It is pictured as a Staff and means – The Essence of Authority and Control – with a Tongue that Speaks Words – with the Symbol of the Shepherd's Staff – The Voice of Authority – To Speak with Authority – The Son.

MEM

Original Hebrew Pictograph of WATERS

Mem is the **13th** letter in the Hebrew Aleph-Beyt. It is pictured as Water and means – Liquid – Massive – Chaos – Living Water – Waters.

Please come along with me on a journey to discover the meaning of the Hebrew word Jerusalem. The name Jerusalem is a combination of two Hebrew words. Remember that Hebrew is written from right to left.

SALEM   U   JER

SALEM U JER

Mem Lamed Sheen	VAV	Reysh Yood

The Hebrew letter Vav ו seen in English as the **U**, the fourth letter in the English spelling of Jer-**U**-Salem separates the two Hebrew words spelled (Yood Reysh) and (Sheen Lamed Mem).

The letter Vav ו in conventional Hebrew is also the word *and,* a word that, just as it does in English, connects two things together. We might say "this and that", "apples and oranges", or "love and marriage". Everyone agrees that the second word in Jer U Salem, the Hebrew word Salem means *peace.*

The meaning of Salem is found in the root-verb Sheen, Lamed, Mem, and the word shalom. Shalom means *un-brokenness* and conveys the meaning of completeness or wholeness. How do the Scriptures use this word that indicates wholeness?

The answer is a payment that restores things to their fullness and wholeness. Does the word *propitiation* come to mind?

Salem means *peace* but not perhaps in the way we think it does! The first two letters in Jerusalem are Yood and Reysh.

The two letters Yood ⎣ Reysh 𝔇 compose the Hebrew word translated into English as *fear* or *awe.*

SALEM U JER

Mem Lamed Sheen	Vav	REYSH YOOD

Clearly, Yood  Reysh , the first two letters in Jerusalem, are meant to instill in us a sense of *awe!*

Whatever the nature of the *peace,* prophetically announced by the Hebrew word *shalom* or *salem,* it is going to, when it is fully disclosed, produce *fear* and *awe!*

The conventional meaning of Jerusalem, the meaning the man on the street will report back to you if asked, is that Jerusalem means the "City of Peace." Is this correct?

Let's take a look at the meaning that the LORD has hidden in plain sight in the very letters and numbers that compose the one place on earth that God has put His name on, *Jerusalem.*

The first letter in the Hebrew name Jerusalem is Yood . Yood is pictured as a Hand. It is an arm and a hand doing a mighty deed in order to accomplish a divine mission. The second letter in the Hebrew name Jerusalem is Reysh. Reysh is pictured as a Head. Reysh is a picture of a person who is the leader, the master, the highest, and the Prince.

The translation of the first word in the Hebrew name Jerusalem could not be clearer. God has designed this revelation so that it might not be misunderstood. The first two letters in the Hebrew word Jerusalem announce that God is going to do a mighty work. Yood Reysh announces who is coming in order to do this mighty work.

Reysh is the Prince!

The Reysh or prince sent by the LORD to Yood, accomplishes a mighty purpose.

Prince   Mighty Deed

Who is this Prince of Heaven?

He has a name above every name. His name is Yeshua. He is the only begotten Son of God who has come to Jerusalem in order to do a mighty work — a work He was anointed to accomplish by His Father in Heaven.

He is Yeshua Ha-Mashiach! What do you suppose this mighty work is?

The answer is found in the picture meaning of the Hebrew word Salem, the second word in the name of Jerusalem. Before we look at the picture meaning of Salem, we need to touch on the meaning of the third letter in the Hebrew word Jerusalem, the letter Vav.

In conventional Hebrew, the letter Vav means *and*. It is the letter in Hebrew that is pictured as an iron nail or a wooden hook. The iron nail and the wooden hook picture joining two things together, creating a connection between two things that are separated from each other.

It also has the meaning of making secure, as pictured by holding something up. We will return to the picture of the iron nail after we discover the picture meaning of Salem, the Hebrew word that is translated into English as *peace*.

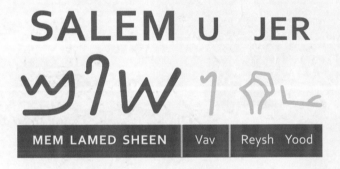

SALEM	U	JER
MEM LAMED SHEEN	Vav	Reysh Yood

The three letters in the Hebrew word Salem, the last three pictures in JeruSALEM are as follows:

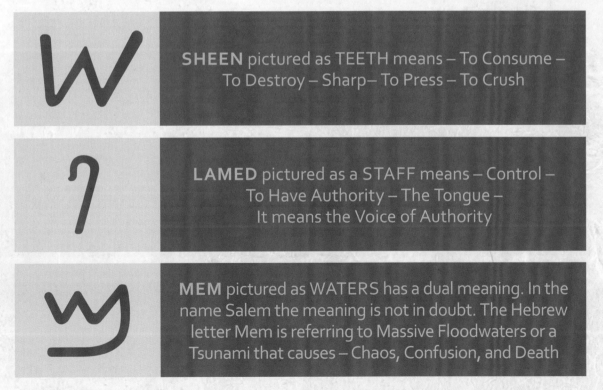

SHEEN pictured as TEETH means – To Consume – To Destroy – Sharp– To Press – To Crush

LAMED pictured as a STAFF means – Control – To Have Authority – The Tongue – It means the Voice of Authority

MEM pictured as WATERS has a dual meaning. In the name Salem the meaning is not in doubt. The Hebrew letter Mem is referring to Massive Floodwaters or a Tsunami that causes – Chaos, Confusion, and Death

Who is the "Controlling Authority connected with Massive Chaos"?

It could only be referring to one person.

Who is the one person causing chaos, confusion, and death?

It is the evil prince of the power of the air; the ruler of this present world who only rules to destroy mankind and make war with the Lord God of Heaven.

Who is the only one with the power and authority to vanquish and destroy the Prince of Chaos and Confusion?

There is only one candidate, and His name is Yeshua Ha-Mashiach. The Prince announced in the first two letters of Jerusalem. The Prince who has come to vanquish death and secure for us, by means of an iron nail and a wooden hook or cross, the one thing that man cannot accomplish on his own — salvation through redemption.

Jerusalem is a prophecy that was partially fulfilled when Yeshua Ha-Mashiach came to earth the first time, as a suffering servant to destroy the works of the Devil.

Jerusalem is a billboard God created and protected, in order that all might read the glorious message of Yeshua the Messiah who came to pay the penalty for the sins of man and to defeat Satan the enemy of our soul.

Jerusalem also announces the *second coming* of Yeshua. He will set up His kingdom in Jerusalem on this earth, and He will reign with a rod of iron for 1000 years.

Jerusalem will only become the City of Peace when it is ruled by the Prince of Peace. When the Prince of Peace comes a second time, He will utterly destroy the already defeated kingdom of this world. A kingdom ruled by the devil and his army of fallen angels and demons.

Would you like to know when this is going to happen? Is the answer revealed in the numeric meaning of Jerusalem? Is there a message hidden in the name of Jerusalem that is finally, in these last days, about to be disclosed?

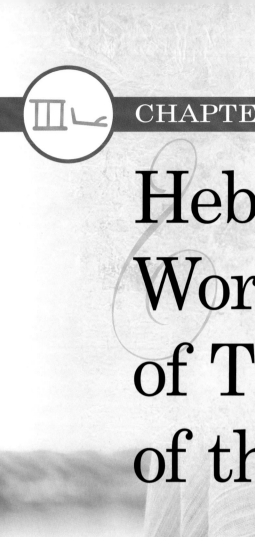

CHAPTER 18

Hebrew Word Study of The Name of the LORD

LORD

English Translation

YHVH

Literal Hebrew

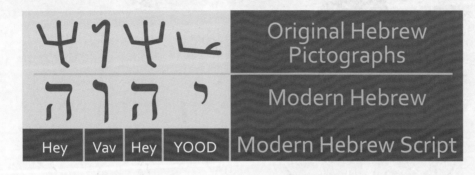

	Original Hebrew Pictographs
	Modern Hebrew
Hey | Vav | Hey | YOOD	Modern Hebrew Script

First Mention:

GENESIS 2:4

These are the generations of the heavens and of the earth when they were created, in the day that the Lord God made the earth and the heavens

Introduction: The Scriptures tell us to fear the LORD and think about His name. Let's begin by reading a unique promise that has been made to those who take the time and make the effort to think about the name of the LORD.

In **the Old Testament book of Malachi** we read the following:

MALACHI 3:16

Then they that feared the LORD spake often one to another: and the LORD hearkened, and heard it, and a book of remembrance was written before him for them that feared the LORD,
and that thought upon his name.

What does the ancient prophetic text, the Scriptures we refer to as the Old Testament, tell us to do with the name of the LORD?

The title LORD, capital L O R D, is displayed almost 7000 times in the Old Testament. As we read the Scriptures, we notice that there are scores of themes that just keep reoccurring which are directly connected to the name of the LORD.

There is not a name of a place or any other person's name that shows up more often in the English translation of the Bible then the title LORD.

There are hundreds of verses that could be used to demonstrate the importance of His name. The Scriptures are packed with verses that instruct us in the ways we are to use His name.

Below are a few samples for you to consider, in order that we might answer this simple question.

How are we to treat the name of the LORD?

We are not to take the name of the LORD in vain. In the literal Hebrew what we know as the third commandment actually informs Israel that His name is meant to bring about atonement, salvation, and life.

To misuse His name is the same as mischaracterizing the person represented by the name and, by so doing, to undue His purposes.

This is why the LORD is *jealous* of His name, as we are told in **Isaiah 42:8.**

The Scriptures tell us to *declare* the name of the LORD throughout the earth. **Exodus 9:16**

The Scriptures tell us that His name is to be *published.* **Deuteronomy 32:3**

His name is to be *glorified.* **1 Chronicles 16:8-10**

We are to *give thanks* to the LORD. **Psalms 92:1**

We are to *come against our enemies* in the name of the LORD.
1 Samuel 17:45

We are to *praise* the name of the LORD. **Psalms 113:3**

In **Isaiah 47:4** and in dozens of Scriptures we discover that the LORD is our *salvation and our redeemer.*

There are hundreds of other verses that bear witness to the praise, honor, and glory due His name. There are scores of verses that instruct us to lift up His name, to publish it, and to declare it throughout the earth.

There is even a special promise made to those who fear the LORD and meditate upon the meaning of His name.

But do you know what there is NOT?

There is no place in the Bible where we are told to *hide* his name, to keep His name a secret, or to substitute His name for another name.

His name is written in the original Hebrew Scriptures almost 7000 times; no other name even comes close. There is nothing as important as His name!

So, here is the big question: What is His name?

If His name brings life, then as a poor sinner seeking life, don't you want to know His name?

Have you ever wondered *why* His name is not found in the Greek and English translations of the Scriptures?

Is His name being purposely hidden?

Many Christians do not realize that the English word "LORD", that is capital LORD, is simply a title. LORD is not a name. The title LORD appears nearly 7000 times in the ancient prophetic Hebrew Scriptures, which Christians call the Old Testament.

Almost 7000 times the true name of the one given the title LORD is covered up and hidden from our view.

What is his name, and what does it mean?

The answer is found in the original Hebrew Scriptures that we call the Old Testament. Those sacred Scriptures declare that His name is YHVH. Did YHVH ever instruct us to hide His name or substitute another name for His name?

The answer is *no.*

YHVH wants His name declared to the entire world.

It is true that His name is sacred, but it is also a name He wanted to be declared and published.

Do you know why?

The answer is that the four letters in the name YHVH reveal a mysterious and glorious message.

In fact, His name heralds the most amazing message to ever be revealed to mankind.

The name YHVH is a prophetic harbinger we are meant to understand.

Throughout the Old Testament, the name of YHVH declares that something is coming, something amazing to behold!

When it is finally revealed and you look for it and behold it, I mean actually see it, then Salvation has come to Israel and the entire world.

Unless, of course, you're blind and full of unbelief.

Or, unless the prophecy has been hidden from you and you have no idea what it means.

The key, that unlocks the meaning of the name YHVH, can be clearly seen in the very letters that are also in the original Hebrew pictures and numbers.

This picture and number language, that was embedded in the text from the very beginning, declares the prophetic meaning of YHVH. To those who are interested in how to pronounce his name, but have no idea what the name means, I would ask the following question:

Have you ever considered that YHVH may not be interested in revealing how His name is pronounced, since He has not given us the means to figure it out. But, instead He wants us to understand what His name means?

The simple truth is that YHVH is a *blazing prophecy,* and trying to figure out how to pronounce His name was simply not His purpose in disclosing His name.

We are meant to know what His name means, and we should be spending our time meditating on the message. It is the greatest revelation to ever be disclosed to mankind. Could it be that the name is purposely unpronounceable because YHVH wants you to discover the magnificent message of *redemption* and *salvation* declared by each letter of His revealed name?

If YHVH contains a message, then let's discover what it means.

You don't have to be a Hebrew language scholar, a rabbi, or a man of letters to see the message that is in plain sight in the four pictographs YHVH.

His name was deliberately written so that a small child could see it and at the precise moment in time the *seeing* becomes *understanding.* Our Heavenly Father delights in playing hide and seek with His children. And, His most profound revelation has been openly declared in the conventional Hebrew language. It was also hidden in plain sight, to be discovered at precisely the right time.

Is this the time?

The lifting of the blindness and the unveiling of the truth is happening around the world in these last days. Could the revelation of the meaning of YHVH be the centerpiece of the unveiling that is sweeping the world?

It is my great privilege to reveal to you what the name YHVH actually means in the pictures and numbers of the Hebrew language. Again, let me remind you that the Hebrew language is a pictographic language, and it is also a numeric language.

This is not something that has been added to the language, it was present at the very moment it was given as a gift to Adam in the Garden of Eden. The language we call Hebrew, the language that God calls the *pure language*, is the language of the Garden of Eden. This pure language has been preserved by God supernaturally in order to communicate His message of salvation and redemption to mankind.

LORD	English Translation
YHVH	Literal Hebrew

		Original Hebrew Pictographs		
		Modern Hebrew		
Hey	Vav	Hey	YOOD	Modern Hebrew Script

Translation of each Picture/Letter in the Hebrew Word YHVH

YOOD		Original Hebrew Pictograph of HAND

Yood is the **10th** letter in the Hebrew Aleph-Beyt. It is pictured as a Hand and means - A Mighty Deed - To Make - Divine Deed.

HEY — Original Hebrew Pictograph to BEHOLD

Hey is the **5th** letter in the Hebrew Aleph-Beyt. It is pictured as a Man with Hands raised to the Heavens and means – Paying Attention to what Follows – Something is going to be Revealed – It Pictures an Unfolding – To Look Upon and Behold – The Holy Spirit is the Gracious Revelator – A picture of the Holy Spirit Giving and us Receiving Revelation – To Reveal – The Revealer – Look – Behold – The Holy Spirit.

The fact that it is mentioned twice in a four-letter Hebrew word is significant. The meaning of receiving revelation is multiplied in importance as it is used twice. Whatever this is, is very important!

VAV — Original Hebrew Pictograph of a NAIL

Vav is the **6th** letter in the Hebrew Aleph-Beyt. It is pictured as a Nail and means To Add – To Secure – To Join Together – To Make Secure –To Bind Together – To Create a Connection between two things that are Separated from each other – Wooden Hook – Wooden Peg – To it means Hold Up – Iron Nail

HEY — Original Hebrew Pictograph to BEHOLD

Hey is the **5th** letter in the Hebrew Aleph-Beyt. It is pictured as a man lifing his hands to Heaven and means Paying Attention to what Follows – Something is going to be Revealed – It Pictures an Unfolding – To Look Upon and Behold – The Holy Spirit is the Gracious Revelator –

It is a picture of the Holy Spirit Giving and us Receiving Revelation –
To Reveal – The Revealer – Look – Behold – The Holy Spirit.

The fifth letter in the sacred name of YHVH is **Hey**. This is the second time the letter Hey is used in the sacred name of YHVH. And, as we indicated above, it is a picture of a man lifting up his hands to the heavens.

Hey means to reveal, to behold, or to look. The meaning of Hey can include fifth doing the revealing or it can indicate receiving revelation. The letter Hey is often used to indicate the presence and work of the Holy Spirit. In which case, it indicates the illuminating, revealing, and disclosing the work of the Holy Spirit.

Let's simply assemble the pictures and see what they reveal.

Hebrew is a verb or action first language, as compared to English, which is a noun first language.

So, let's translate this prophetic picture language of YHVH into plain English.

Picture Translation of the YHVH Our Creator

The clearest pictorial translation of YHVH, the Sacred Name of God is:

Behold the Hand!   Behold the Nail!

Translation of each Number in the Hebrew Word YHVH

Now let's examine the numbers embedded under each of the four letters in the name of YHVH - the sacred name that has been hidden behind the name LORD over 6000 times in Holy Scripture.

The meaning of these numbers is based exclusively on how these numbers are used in the Scriptures. The Scriptures themselves are the second witness to the meaning of both the pictures and the numbers embedded in each of the 22 letters in the Hebrew Alpha-Beyt.

YOOD   10   Ordinal Perfection

Perfection of Divine Order – Completeness of Order – Testimony – The Law –Responsibility

Notice how the picture of the hand doing a divine work and the meaning of the number 10 are complimentary.

Notice Ordinal Perfection notifies us that there is a Divinely Appointed Sequence of events that will unfold at exactly the appointed Time. Yood, or the number 10, is a prophetic alert that there is going to be a sequence of events ordained by the Heavenly Father that will unfold on the earth in order to conclude a divine work.

HEY   5   Grace

God's Goodness – What Follows Creation – Pentateuch – Divine Strength – Unmerited Favor – Grace

VAV   6   Number of Man

Man's World – Enmity with God – Weakness of man – Manifestation of Sin – Evils of Satan – Falling short – Preservation Imperfection – Number of men without God – Labor – Sorrow –Secular Completeness – Sixth

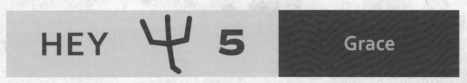

HEY   5   Grace

God's Goodness – What Follows Creation – Pentateuch – Divine Strength – Unmerited Favor – Grace

Translation of the Number
Meaning of the Word YHVH

Yood 10 After a sequence of events at exactly
the right Divinely Appointed Time **Hey 5**
The LORD will show Grace and Favor **Vav 6**
To Fallen Mankind **Hey 5** as a manifestation
of Divine Grace!

And, how will we know when this season of divine grace is upon us?

What will be the sign of this divine intervention that comes from
the gracious heart of our Heavenly Father at exactly the right time,
manifesting unmerited grace and mercy?

How will we know when the prophecy is fulfilled in time and space?

The picture language tells us.

We are told to: *Behold the Hand! Behold the Nail!*

The prophetic puzzle purposely placed in the name God revealed to man,
the name YHVH, can now be fully understood. We see the Savior lifted up
on a Cross — with outstretched hands secured by an iron nail held up on
a wooden cross.

This pictorial revelation is set forth with each utterance and each textual
reference to YHVH, throughout the entire ancient prophetic text of the
Hebrew Scriptures, that we call the Old Testament.

You can hardly find a page in the original Old Testament Hebrew
Scriptures, where the prophetic harbinger being revealed in the name of
YHVH, is not present.

Replace the title LORD in your English Bible with the name YHVH, and
you can to can hear as well as see the accomplishment of God's gracious
plan for mankind.

Now, we see the Messiah, who came to save mankind, echoing across the prophetic pages of the Old Testament just as Yeshua said, for those who searched the Scriptures.

You can now see what a marvel it is to meditate on the Name of YHVH.

You can also see the prophetic harbinger displayed from the moment of the fall of creation when God revealed His name as YHVH.

The name echoes across the ages and finds its fulfillment on a cruel wooden cross where Yeshua accomplished our salvation.

What do we see when we cast our gaze upon the Cross of Calvary?

We see the unfolding of the meaning and message of the sacred name of YHVH. We see the hand willingly grasping the iron nail. We see the fulfillment of a divine sequence of events designed by the Creator of the universe in order that we might experience eternal life.

Consider the messages that this beacon broadcasts each time it is observed:

YHVH – Look for the *hand* and the *nail.* When you see it salvation has come to Israel and the entire world.

YHVH – At the *divinely appointed* time salvation has come to mankind.

YHVH – A *saving grace* has been freely given to all men who look upon and behold the hand and the nail with eyes of faith and trusting hearts.

YHVH is our salvation and Yeshua is His name.

Behold Yeshua Ha-Maschiach!
Now you know the meaning of *salvation* hidden in plain sight and found on almost every page of the ancient prophetic Scriptures.

YHVH -Behold the Hand, Behold the Nail!

CHAPTER 19

Hebrew Word Study of Bless

BLESS

English Translation

BE-RUKH

Literal Hebrew

			Original Hebrew Pictographs
			Modern Hebrew
Kaf	Reysh	Beyt	Modern Hebrew Script

Introduction: The dictionary defines the word *bless* as "to consecrate or sanctify by a religious rite; make or pronounce holy". Another meaning of bless is to request of God the bestowal of divine favor on a person, place, or thing. It also means to extol as holy and to glorify.

Probably the most well-known use of the Hebrew word for *bless* is located in Genesis:

> *And I will bless them that bless thee, and curse him that curseth thee: and in thee shall all families of the earth be blessed.*
>
> ## GENESIS 12:3

It is interesting that the most well-known time the word bless is used in the Scriptures is in relationship to Abraham, the one to whom the promises were made. The promises were made to Abraham and his seed. And, it was from Abraham that the genealogical progression would gloriously conclude in the coming of the promised Messiah. The Messiah was destined to make atonement for fallen and sinful mankind. The blessing given to Abraham would have its final and ideal fulfillment in the salvation of the world. Keep this in mind as we discover the amazing picture that is embedded in the Hebrew word translated into English as *bless.* You can read about this unconditional promise in the Genesis, 22:17-18.

Translation of each Picture/Letter in the Hebrew Word Bless

BEYT — Original Hebrew Pictograph of a TENT **or** HOUSE

Beyt is the **2nd** letter in the Hebrew Aleph-Beyt. Beyt is pictured as a Tent or House and means – House – Tent – Son – Family – Dwelling Place – physical Tent or Body – Inside – Within – the First Letter in the Torah to identify the Son of God.

REYSH — Original Hebrew Pictograph of PRINCE

Reysh is the **20th** letter in the Hebrew Aleph-Beyt. Reysh is pictured as the Head Person and means – A Person – The Head – The Highest – Leader – The Sum – The Supreme – The First – The Most Important – The Top – Master – Prince.

KAF — Original Hebrew Pictograph of PALM OF HAND

Kaf is the **11th** letter in the Hebrew Aleph-Beyt. Kaf is pictured as an Open Hand Palm Out and means – To Cover – A Covering – To Open – To Allow – Atonement.

Pictographic Translation of Bless

Beyt ⬠ ⊓ **Reysh** 👑 ⟩ The Prince who comes out of the House. In other words, the beyt reysh is the Son. The Son is in view as we discover the ideal picture meaning embedded in the three Hebrew letters. It is the Son who is the Prince of Heaven, coming to make atonement.

Kaf ✋ ⫴ He is coming to cover the sin that keeps us from fellowship with our Heavenly Father.

Numeric Translation of Bless

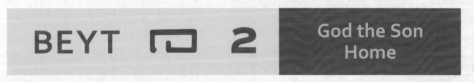

Difference (Good or Evil) – Division – Living Word – Second – To Come Alongside – To Hinder – To Come Alongside for Help – The Son of God

10 X 20 – Magnified Ordinal Perfection & Redemption – Redemption of Body and Soul Multiplied by Ordinal Perfection – Accomplished by the Son of God – Sufficient to Accomplish a Purpose – Ransom that is both Efficient and Sufficient to Reclaim what was Lost – To Accomplish Redemption

10 X 2 – Magnified Ordinal Perfection & Redemption

The Summary of the Numeric Translation of Bless

The Hebrew word bless is crowned with the number 2. Clearly, the Son of God, the second person in the divine Trinity, is in view. His mission is to come along side to rescue us, to redeem us, and present us to His father without spot or wrinkle. Our sins have been paid in full by the amazing sacrifice of the Son of God, our Savior, the Lord Jesus Christ.

CHAPTER 20

Hebrew Word Study of Created

CREATED

English Translation

BARA

Literal Hebrew

⋎	◻	⌐	Original Hebrew Pictographs
א	ב	ר	Modern Hebrew
Aleph	Beyt	Reysh	Modern Hebrew Script

First Mention:

GENESIS 1:1

*In the beginning God **created** the heaven and the earth.*

Introduction: The biblical revelation is that *all matter* came "from nothing" as a result of God speaking all things into existence. The Word of God made all things. The concept that matter comes "from nothing" is called creation-ex-nihilo in the Latin, more directly "creation out of nothing".

The biblical view is that in the beginning there was God, and all creation has its beginning in Him.

God's purpose in creation is revelation.

What is it that God is revealing?

The answer is found in the pictographic translation of creation.

Translation of each Picture/Letter in the Hebrew Word Creation

BEYT — Original Hebrew Pictograph of a TENT or HOUSE

Beyt is the **2nd** letter in the Hebrew Aleph-Beyt. It is pictured as a Tent or House and means – House – Tent – Son – Family – Dwelling Place – The Physical Tent or Body – Inside – Within – the First Letter in the Torah that identifies the Son of God.

Original Hebrew Pictograph of PRINCE

Reysh is the **20th** letter in the Hebrew Aleph-Beyt is pictured as the Head Person and it means – A Person – The Head – The Highest – Leader – The Sum The Supreme – The First – The Most Important – The Top Master – Prince.

The person who comes out of the house is the son. The pictographic meaning of Beyt Reysh is the son. Beyt Reysh is *Bar* – as in Bar Jonah, the son of Jonah.

The question is whose son?

The answer is found in the last pictograph in the Hebrew pictographs that reveal **creation**. The answer is — God the Father!

Original Hebrew Pictograph of an OX

Aleph is the **1st** letter in the Hebrew Aleph-Beyt. It is pictured as an Ox and means – Strong Leader – First – God the Father.

Picture Translation of Creator
Without apology God ⊽ reveals the pictorial meaning
of creation by revealing that it was accomplished
by the word remove pictogram of His Son
the BARA the
SON OF GOD

The Scriptures declare that Son of God spoke the heavens and earth, and all that is in them, into existence!

JOHN 1:1-3

In the beginning was the Word, and the Word was with God, and the Word was God.

The same was in the beginning with God.

All things were made by him; and without him was not anything made that was made.

Translation of each Number in the Hebrew Word Created

BEYT 2 — God the Son– HOME

Difference (Good or Evil) – Division – Living Word – Second – To come Alongside – To Hinder – To come Alongside for Help – The Son of God

REYSH 200 — SUFFICIENCY of God & Insufficiency of Man

10 X 20 – **Magnified Ordinal Perfection & Redemption** – Redemption of Body and Soul Multiplied by Ordinal Perfection – Accomplished by the Son of God – Sufficient to Accomplish a Purpose – Ransom that is both Efficient and Sufficient To Reclaim what was Lost – To Accomplish Redemption

ALEPH 1 — God the Father

Deity – Unity – Complete Self Sufficiency – Independence – The First – Indivisible – The First Cause of Everything Else

Translation of the Number Meaning of the Word Created

God the Son made a home for us at the direction of and in full cooperation with His Father. The Father willed it, and the Son accomplished it by means of a sinless creation. A creation designed in order to direct the first man, Adam, and all his children after him, to love their Creator with all their hearts.

Adam failed the test of love and loyalty. Through Adam we have all sinned and are now living in a fallen corrupt world that has been marred and mangled by sin.

It is into this fallen creation which now teams with sin and death, the Creator has come to call sinners to repent and put their faith and trust in Him. And, in so doing, they will receive entrance into another home, one that is incorruptible and will never pass away.

ROMANS 5:19

For as by one man's disobedience many were made sinners,
so by the obedience of one shall many be made righteous.

I TIMOTHY 1:15

This is a faithful saying, and worthy of all acceptation, that Christ Jesus came into the world to save sinners; of whom I am chief.

JOHN 14:1-3

Let not your heart be troubled: ye believe in God, believe also in me.

In my Father's house are many mansions: if it were not so, I would have told you. I go to prepare a place for you.

And if I go and prepare a place for you, I will come again, and receive you unto myself; that where I am, there ye may be also.

The Creator is Calling! Are you listening?

CHAPTER 21

Hebrew Word Study of Blood

BLOOD

English Translation

DAM

Literal Hebrew

	Original Hebrew Pictographs
	Modern Hebrew
Mem | Dalet	Modern Hebrew Script

First Mention

GENESIS 4:10

And he said, What hast thou done? the voice of thy brother's blood crieth unto me from the ground.

Introduction: The dictionary defines blood as the fluid that circulates in the principal vascular system of human beings and other vertebrates. In humans blood consists of plasma in which the red blood cells, white blood cells, and platelets are suspended. Blood is the vital principle of life.

How important is blood? The Scriptures provide the answer.

LEVITICUS 17:11

For the life of the flesh is in the blood: and I have given it to you upon the altar to make an atonement for your souls: for it is the blood that maketh an atonement for the soul.

REVELATION 1:5

And from Jesus Christ, who is the faithful witness, and the first begotten of the dead, and the prince of the kings of the earth. Unto him that loved us, and washed us from our sins in his own blood,

Translation of each Picture/Letter
in the Hebrew Word Blood

Original Hebrew Pictograph of a PATHWAY or DOOR

Dalet the **4th** letter in the Hebrew Aleph-Beyt. It is pictured as a Pathway or Door and means – Pathway – Doorway – Gate – Place of Decision – Entrance to Life or Death –Moving into Something – Moving out of Something – To Open up – A Place where Change can take place – Door.

Original Hebrew Pictograph of a WATERS

Mem is the **13th** letter in the Hebrew Aleph-Beyt. It is pictured as Water and means – Liquid – Mighty Waters like the Ocean – Massive as the Waves of the Sea – Chaotic and Destructive like a Tsunami – Water coming down like a Stream – Rain Water that make the Desert Bloom – The Word of God that brings Life – Living Water – Waters.

Picture Translation of Blood

The Hebrew word *blood* is a stellar example of the power invested by virtue of the pictures into the Hebrew Aleph-Beyt. It is said that a picture paints a thousand words. In the case of the word blood, the picture God has painted in this simple two-picture word will fill eternity with its glory.

At the elementary level, God has given us a simple understanding of blood.

Blood is the liquid that travels through the pathways in our body.

Translation of each Number in the Hebrew Word Blood

BLOOD
English Translation

ש	ד	Original Hebrew Pictographs
Mem	Dalet	Modern Hebrew Script
40	4	Modern Hebrew Numbers

DALET ד 4 — Creation

Creation – The World – God's Creative works –
The Fourth Thing – The World – Four Elements –
Four Regions of Earth – Four Seasons –
Four divisions of Day – Four in Contrast to Seven –
Earth (4) vs. Heaven (7) – The Fourth Thing –
First Number that Can be Divided –
Material World that had a Beginning – Creation.

MEM ש 40 — Probation & Testing

Trials – Probation – Chastisement but not Judgment – Action of Grace
resulting in Revival – Magnified Renewal – An Extended
Period of Rule or Dominion – Grace multiplied by Eternity
(5 X 8) – Working out a gracious Purpose that
has everlasting Consequences – Probationary Period
that results in Renewal of God's Goodness –
Follows Creation – Divine Strength –
Unmerited Favor – Grace.

Translation of the Number
Messianic Meaning of the Word Blood

Is Blood something God created in order to demonstrate His grace? A grace that results in revival?

There is one more revelation in the picture and number meaning of the Hebrew word for blood. Although, we do not have space in this article to consider this exhaustive topic, I can give you a hint that will allow you to begin turning this fact over in your mind, for the purpose of doing some serious meditation and consideration.

The disclosure is simply that the letters Dalet and Mem are the last two letters in the Hebrew name Aleph Dalet Mem — the name Adam.

ADAM

ש	ת	⟱	Original Hebrew Pictographs
Mem	Dalet	Aleph	Modern Hebrew Script
40	4	1	Modern Hebrew Numbers

The word blood composes two-thirds of Adam's name.

Do you see the Messianic message?

In order to understand it, we need to look at the sum of Adam's name. That sum is forty-five (40 + 4+ 1 =45).

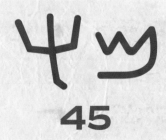

45

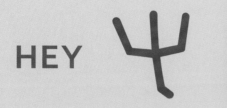

HEY

God's Goodness – What Follows Creation
– Pentateuch – Divine Strength –
Unmerited Favor – Grace

Adam was put on  40 probation but has failed the test.

What follows are sin and corruption that lead to death.

God the Son intervened and changed the outcome from death

to life by His matchless 5 Grace!

The Messianic implications of this are staggering, when you consider
that one of the names identified with the Messiah is Adam. Yeshua Ha
Mashiach is the *last Adam*.

And they sung a new song, saying, Thou art worthy to take the book, and to open the seals thereof: for thou wast slain, and hast redeemed us to God by thy blood out of every kindred, and tongue, and people, and nation;

REVELATION 5:9

But Christ being come an high priest of good things to come, by a greater and more perfect tabernacle, not made with hands, that is to say, not of this building; Neither by the blood of goats and calves, but by his own blood he entered in once into the holy place, having obtained eternal redemption for us. For if the blood of bulls and of goats, and the ashes of an heifer sprinkling the unclean, sanctifieth to the purifying of the flesh: How much more shall the blood of Christ, who through the eternal Spirit offered himself without spot to God, purge your conscience from dead works to serve the living God? And for this cause he is the mediator of the new testament, that by means of death, for the redemption of the transgressions that were under the first testament, they which are called might receive the promise of eternal inheritance.

HEBREWS 9:11-15

CHAPTER 22

Hebrew Word Study of Father

FATHER

English Translation

AB

Literal Hebrew

		Original Hebrew Pictographs
		Modern Hebrew
Beyt	Aleph	Modern Hebrew Script

First Mention

GENESIS 2:24

*Therefore shall a man leave his father and his mother,
and shall cleave unto his wife: and they shall be one flesh.*

Introduction: The Hebrew word for *father* is Ab (or Av). Contrary to popular belief, the word Abba does not show up anywhere in the Hebrew Old Testament.

The Hebrew word for father is everywhere written as AB. The two-letter word Aleph Beyt is in the Hebrew Scripture to describe the Father.

There is some controversy surrounding the word "Abba" and its origins. Many believe this was an Aramaic way to express a familiar title equivalent to "daddy". However, some evidence suggests otherwise.

The thought of Abba being an Aramaic way of saying "daddy" was the suggestion of a 20th century scholar, Jeremias, and it was intended to be only a suggestion.

The New Testament term ABBA ($\alpha\beta\beta\alpha$ in the Greek New Testament–always connected with "the Father") was thought to be "partnered" with the term "pater" (father) to help the Greeks understand that Abba meant father. But, it seems strongly out of place. Especially, in light of the fact that in English Abba is transliterated, while Pater is translated.

Regardless of the etymological evidence, if you look at the Hebrew picture and numbers for the four letter word Abba and compare it to the two letter word Ab, you will immediately discover the difference of the two words. At the root, they do not mean the same thing. Since we are interested in what God has revealed, not what man has corrupted and accepted no matter how popular it has become, we will limit our investigation of the word father to the original two-letter Hebrew word for father.

Modern Hebrew today uses the word Abba as an intimate reference to father (daddy or papa). It is possible that oral tradition has carried this down from native Hebrew speakers throughout the generations.

Let's look at the original Hebrew as it relates to AB. In the conventional Hebrew, father is a word we all understand.

If someone is the father, he has children. A father is the head of a family.

We think of God as the father of His people. It is a word that presupposes relationships that connect one person who is the head or chief person to other people by natural birth or adoption of national kinship.

Translation of each Picture/Letter in the Hebrew Word Father

Aleph is the **1st** letter in the Hebrew Aleph-Beyt.
It is pictured as an Ox and means – a Strong Leader –
First – God the Father.

BEYT

Original Hebrew Pictograph of a TENT or HOUSE

Beyt is the **2nd** letter in the Hebrew Aleph-Beyt.
It is pictured as a Tent or House and means – House – Tent – Son – Family – Dwelling Place – the Physical Tent or Body – Inside – Within – First Letter in the Torah that identifies the Son of God.

Picture Translation Of Father

Aleph is the first letter in the Hebrew Aleph-Beyt. The literal picture is that of an ox. The meaning would have been clear in the original Hebrew, as the ox was the symbol of both strength and leadership. The ox leads the cows and calves in its herd to safe pastures and protects them from predators.

Beyt is the second letter in the Hebrew Aleph-Beyt. The picture is literally of a house or tent.

Put the two letters together and you have the ▽ *Strong Leader and Protector* ⌐◻ *of the House or Household.*

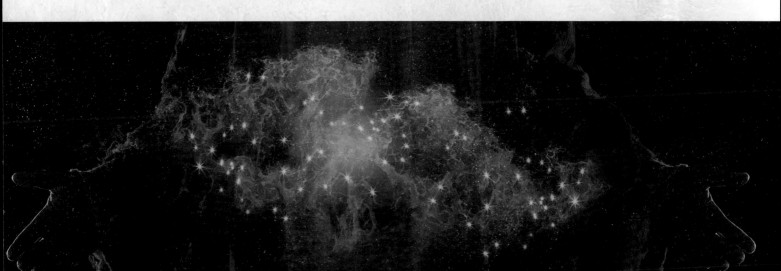

Translation of each Number in the Hebrew Word Father

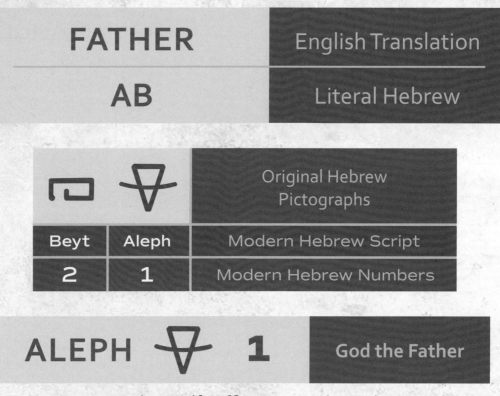

FATHER	English Translation
AB	Literal Hebrew

		Original Hebrew Pictographs
Beyt	Aleph	Modern Hebrew Script
2	1	Modern Hebrew Numbers

ALEPH 1 God the Father

Deity – Unity – Complete Self Sufficiency – Independence – The First – Indivisible – The First Cause of everything else

BEYT 2 God the Son- HOME

Difference (Good or Evil) – Division – Living Word – Second – To Come Alongside – to Hinder – To Come Alongside for Help – the Son of God

It appears, at first glance, that little has been added to the idea of a father who has a son. The father in mind is the father of a son not a daughter. That narrows it down but does not really answer the question as to why the child must be a son. Why not be the father of a daughter or a son and a daughter?

God designed this word to have an ideal and a Messianic meaning.

We can see ▽ **1 God the Father.**

We can see ⊓ **2 God the Son**.

Is there something else God wants us to see - something that would be corrupted if we simply went along with conventional and traditional thought and ignored the literal Hebrew word for father?

The answer is YES!

The summary of the numeric number, that is the number of the Aleph-Beyt, solves the riddle.

▽ **1 God the Father** + ⊓ **2 God the Son**

Could it be any simpler to understand?

1 + 2 = 3

GIMEL	L	3	Holy Spirit pictured as a CAMEL

Divine Perfection – The Trinity Completeness – Solid – Substantial – The Entirety – God the Holy Spirit.

To be clear, in Hebrew if you were asked what number Aleph and Beyt was you would be told that it is the number 3 expressed as Gimel.

The house of the father has a third resident which makes the household complete and perfect.

And who is that person?

None other than the Holy Spirit.

This important revelation would have been completely missed, and the theological masterpiece of God's numeric revelation about

Himself would have been lost had we not used the original Hebrew word for father.

A word that in the conventional phonetic Hebrew simply means *father,* but when supported by the pictograph of the strong leader of the *house,* the theological messaging shows up in the numbers and inform us that there is a third member of the household - the Holy Spirit.

This revelation is meant to open up the mind and heart in order to unlock a spiritual message. A message that tells us that we can only be welcomed into our Heavenly Father's home by a direct and singular revelation from the Holy Spirit.

There is no salvation, no redemption, no atonement for sin, no forgiveness, and no grace apart from the work done on our behalf on the cross of Calvary by the only begotten Son of God.

This is something to think about the next time you pray to God the Father.

APPENDIX A
Expanded Pictographic Content of the Ancient Hebrew Aleph-Beyt

ALEPH		Pictured as an Ox. It means of a strong leader, the first, God the Father, the beginning, the head of the family.
BEYT		Pictured as the floor plan of the Tent. It means of the house, family, dwelling place, or inside, and is the first letter that identifies the Son of God.
GIMEL		Pictured as a Camel. It means to lift up, to lift up with pride, exaltation, or to toil, and can be a picture of the Holy Spirit.
DALET		Pictured as a Door. It means of a doorway, to move in or out of something, a place of decision, an entrance to life or death, a place where change can take place.
HEY		Pictured as a Man with his Arms Lifted up to the Heavens. It means of behold, to reveal, to look upon, to pay attention to what follows, or the Holy Spirit as the revelator.
VAV		Pictured as a wooden Hook or a metal Nail. It means to secure, to join together, to bind together, or to connect two things together that are separated from one another.
ZAYIN		Pictured as a Sharp Tool. It means to cut, to cut off, to prune, to harvest, or to pierce.
CHET		Pictured as a Fence. It means of private, cut off or separated, protected, a place of refuge, a sanctuary, or an inner room.
TET		Pictured as a coiled Snake. It means to surround, to entwine, to encircle, to ensnare, to entrap.
YOOD		Pictured as a Hand. It means to work, a mighty deed, to accomplish a divine deed or purpose.

KAF	Pictured as the Palm of a Hand. It means to cover, to open, to allow, or to atone.
LAMED	Pictured as a Staff. It means to control, to shepherd, to have authority, or the voice of authority.
MEM	Pictured as Water. Has the meaning of liquid. Can be mighty chaotic waves of destruction like a tsunami, or gentle waters that come down from the heavens and bring life. It can mean the Living Waters and the Word of God that brings life.
NOON	Pictured as a Fish or Sprout. It means activity and life.
SAMECH	Pictured as a Prop. It means to support, to assist, to prop, or to twist slowly.
AYIN	Pictured as an Eye. It means to see, to know, or to experience.
PEY	Pictured as an open Mouth. It means to speak, to open, or a word.
TSADE	Pictured as a Fishhook. It means to catch, to harvest, to strongly desire, to be unable to escape, to need, to be just or righteous.
QOOF	Pictured as the Back of the Head. It means behind, the last, or the least.
REYSH	Pictured as the Head. It means a person who is the head, the highest, the supreme, the master, the leader, or the prince.
SHEEN	Pictured as Teeth. It means sharp, to press, to consume, or to destroy. It is the one letter that God uses to identify Himself.
TAV	Pictured as Crossed Wooden Sticks. It means a sign, to seal, or to covenant.

APPENDIX B
Expanded Meanings of the Numbers of the Aleph-Beyt

1	Deity, unity, sufficiency, the first, God the Father.
2	Living Word, God the Son, second person of the Godhead, to come alongside to hinder or to help, difference or division between good or evil.
3	Divine perfection, completeness, lifting up the name of God, God the Holy Spirit.
4	Creation, the world, the material world that had a beginning.
5	Grace, favor not merited, God's goodness, divine strength.
6	Enmity with God, weakness of man, falling short, imperfection, number of man, sorrow, secular completeness.
7	Spiritual completion, completion, good, perfect, God the Father's perfection, the inspiration of the Holy Spirit.
8	Eternity, new creation, new birth, new beginning, first in a new series.
9	Judgement of man, wrath, conclusion of a matter, summation of man's works.
10	Ordinal perfection, perfection of divine order, divinely ordered events, completeness of order, the law.
20	Redemption, concentrated meaning of ordinal perfection, expectancy.

30	Blood of Christ, blood sacrifice, dedication, magnified perfection of divine order marking the right moment.
40	Trials, testing, probation, chastisement but not judgement, grace multiplied by renewal, a probationary period that results in renewal.
50	Work of the Holy Spirit, deliverance followed by rest, grace multiplied, jubilee.
60	Pride.
70	Perfect spiritual order carried out with all spiritual power and significance (7 x 10), punishment and restoration of Israel.
80	Magnified ordinal perfection resulting in eternality (8 x 10), new beginning and new birth.
90	Conclusion of a matter followed by judgement, combination of ordinal perfection and judgement at the conclusion of a series (10 x 9).
100	Children of the promise, God's election of grace, promise.
200	Insufficiency of man, inadequate, lacking what is necessary or required, inability to accomplish a required purpose, deficient, all compared to: the complete sufficiency of God, the adequacy of the eternal, the ransom that is both efficient and sufficient to reclaim what was lost.
300	Signifies the final blood sacrifice made by the perfect Lamb of God, a divinely appointed time connected to the children of promise, election, supernatural victory over enemies including evil and death, the number connected to the death - burial - resurrection of Messiah.
400	A divinely appointed time that will bring about deliverance and renewal, a period of probation to accomplish a divine purpose (40 x 10).